INVITATION TO
VERNACULAR ARCHITECTURE

INVITATION TO
VERNACULAR ARCHITECTURE

A Guide to the Study of
Ordinary Buildings and Landscapes

Thomas Carter and Elizabeth Collins Cromley

THE UNIVERSITY OF TENNESSEE PRESS

KNOXVILLE

The Vernacular Architecture Studies series provides focused investigations into methodological and theoretical issues in the field of vernacular architecture studies. Written by experts in the field with the student, practitioner, and general public in mind, the series will comprise handbooks and historically grounded instructional texts that embody the very latest research from a burgeoning discipline in an accessible, practical form.

Carter, Thomas, 1949–
Invitation to vernacular architecture : a guide to the study of ordinary buildings and landscapes / Thomas Carter and Elizabeth Collins Cromley.—1st ed.
      p. cm. — (Vernacular architecture studies series)
Includes bibliographical references and index.

ISBN 1-57233-331-6 (pbk.: alk. paper)

  1. Vernacular architecture—United States.
  2. Regionalism in architecture—United States.
  3. Architecture and society—United States.
  I. Cromley, Elizabeth C.
 II. Title.
III. Series.

NA705.C38 2005
720'.973—dc22   2004024528

CONTENTS

ILLUSTRATIONS

FOREWORD

Thomas Carter and Elizabeth Collins Cromley's *Invitation to Vernacular Architecture* does more than invite us to study vernacular architecture; it shows us how to do it and what we learn from it. Linking vernacular architecture to the larger endeavor of material culture studies, the authors argue that all human-made objects provide insights into the culture that produced them. The researcher's challenge is to devise a strategy that will enable buildings to reveal their history and meaning.

The ordinariness of vernacular architecture itself can be an impediment to study. Such buildings can be so regionally or numerically commonplace that we do not even see them and select instead the extraordinary as our subject. Even when chosen, typical buildings can be hard to investigate. Where does one begin when there is seemingly nothing written about a prosaic building, builder, or occupant? We begin with the physical building itself.

This book explains how to do that. Demystifying field work, Carter and Cromley explain how to document a building through measured drawings and analysis of the building fabric. Interpretation, not documentation, is the final goal. In order to elicit a building's cultural meaning, the authors further show how to examine the physical and overlooked archival evidence for patterns or points of comparison in terms of time, space, form, style, type, function, and technology. They offer models of interpretation, and show how a mute building can be made to speak.

Carter and Cromley take us step by step through the process of selecting, researching, and deciphering historical architecture. In the end, they give us not only the tools but also an invitation to use them. Their volume launches the first in an educational series published by the University of Tennessee Press and the Vernacular Architecture Forum promoting the study of vernacular architecture. "We hope you will use your imagination to move beyond just descriptions of buildings to interpreting the results," they urge "and will add your own chapters to the ongoing story of vernacular architecture's meanings."

DIANE SHAW
Series Editor,
Vernacular Architecture Studies

ACKNOWLEDGMENTS

We have spent the past twenty-some years learning how to explore the vernacular environment with the help of colleagues in the Vernacular Architecture Forum (VAF). We came to this study from quite different backgrounds. Carter, whose degree is in folklore, started his grad-school investigations in traditional music but discovered buildings about the same time he realized that he was tone-deaf. Cromley took her degree in art history but interested herself in the kinds of social issues about buildings that her grad-school advisers dismissed. For both of us, the early meetings of the Vernacular Architecture Forum provided life-changing lessons. Aspects of buildings glimpsed through art-historical or folklore approaches were not, we discovered, the only things to see. Archaeologists, architectural preservationists, social historians, folklorists, art and architectural historians, anthropologists, planners, conservators, cultural geographers, and those from American studies programs all came to VAF meetings; they all had interesting things to teach one another about the vernacular environment. We were surprised and delighted to discover the variety of ways that these scholars approached buildings, and we found in the VAF a comforting arena in which the issues that concerned us were legitimized. We have never stopped learning from these colleagues, among whom we have also found some of our closest friends.

A few years ago the Board of the Vernacular Architecture Forum decided to expand its publication program beyond the volumes of *Perspectives in Vernacular Architecture* and to pursue additional special topics in the field. This is the first volume in that occasional series. We thought that a book of basic pointers on how to study the vernacular environment would be beneficial, and we thank the board and the University of Tennessee Press for encouraging our project.

Several of our friends on various faculties who were teaching architectural history or preservation courses agreed to "test drive" this book with their students during the autumn of 2002. We are grateful to professors Alison Hoagland, Claire Dempsey, and Catherine Bishir for conveying their students' responses to an earlier version of this book. Our own students also gave us helpful opinions as to what worked and what did not. In addition we thank Martha McNamara, Diane Shaw, Dell Upton, and Gary Stanton for comments on the manuscript and the many improvements they suggested. University of Utah students Collin Tomb, Yoshikazu Kono, and James Gosney helped prepare some of the drawings for publication, and their help is greatly appreciated. Friends were important too, and we want to thank Sarah Sabiston, Bob King, Dwight Butler, Jerry Pocius, Edward Chappell, Gray Read, Camille Wells, Curt Lamb, and many others for being there along the way.

INTRODUCTION

This book is intended as a beginner's guide to vernacular architecture studies. The idea for it came from the classroom. As teachers, we wanted an introductory text for students that would both open their eyes to the world of ordinary buildings and outline a basic method for studying them. It had to be affordable, so it had to be short. And if not simple, the coverage had to be straightforward enough so that students and others encountering this material for the first time could easily use it. Luckily we had a model. When we were talking about what our research guide might look like, James Deetz's pocket-sized *Invitation to Archaeology* immediately came to mind. The book cost $1.45 in the late 1960s and presented readers with a concise but detailed description of how to go about putting archaeology into practice. We honor both book and author in recycling its title and basic approach here. There was nothing we could do about the price.[1]

The study of vernacular architecture is part of a larger scholarly undertaking known as material culture studies.[2] *Material culture* may be defined, following Deetz, as "that segment of [the human] physical environment which is purposely shaped . . . according to culturally dictated plans."[3] Unlike other mammals, humans cannot simply live in nature; rather, we must devise ways of finding and making shelter, clothing and feeding ourselves, and producing the tools needed for survival. In short, people need things—objects, artifacts, however they are referred to—to live in the world, and we make those things, not randomly or by chance, but systematically and intentionally through our culture. Culture is unseen and immaterial, consisting of the ideas, values, and beliefs of a particular social group or society; but it is everywhere within us, shaping our behavior, helping us to choose the right things to say, providing rules for social interaction, and giving us mental blueprints for making the things we need, from bread pans to buildings. Among Americans, for example, people for whom private space is a highly valued commodity, any number of devices—from having your own plate from which to eat, your own drawers for your clothes, your own special chair on which to sit, to even having your own bathroom—can help achieve the goal of privacy. Building separate, detached houses that are spaced far apart in the countryside or separated by just a few feet in urban neighborhoods (fig. 1) would be another way this spirit of individuation is advanced through architecture.[4] We need to remember that the everyday objects we see all around us are indicators of our cultural values. The material world we construct around us is the world that the study of material culture reveals.

If culture determines behavior, and we can see such behavior in the things people make, it is logical that we can also move in the opposite direction, working back from the object in an attempt to explain the ideas, values, and beliefs—the culture—that caused that object to come into being.[5] Archaeologists take this as the central axiom of their discipline since objects are all they have to work with. But others in the academy use material culture as well. Artifact-oriented disciplines such as art history, architectural

Fig. 1. The preference for detached houses in America is visible in these rows of houses from St. Louis, Missouri. While in densely developed cities the older British practice of building continuous rows or terraces of houses was often followed, in less densely developed urban areas and suburbs American builders left gaps between the individual houses, clearly articulating the boundaries of each household's space. Photo by Thomas Carter.

history, folklife studies, historic preservation, cultural landscape studies, industrial arch-aeology, and vernacular architecture studies—the field we are concerned with here—all revolve in their own ways around the study of objects for cultural meaning.

Vernacular architecture studies may in this way be defined as *the study of those human actions and behaviors that are manifest in commonplace architecture.* In the category of commonplace architecture we include individual buildings, assemblages of such buildings, and entire architectural landscapes that serve as primary evidence for our research. The investigative techniques and interpretive theories employed by ver-nacular architecture scholars are those of material culture studies generally, for they center on the ability to find meaning in artifacts. As an academic exercise, the study of material culture is grounded in the physical and material presence of objects—in the case of vernacular architecture, buildings—and relies on the analysis of particular sets of forms and the patterns they make to tell us about human behavior both past and present. Written documents such as books, journals, and court records are used when and where they are available to augment the architectural record. Oral history and ethnographic observation are at times also important to the vernacular architecture researcher. It should be stressed, however, that the field of material culture studies remains artifact-driven, and the investigation and interpretation of buildings and land-scapes play leading roles in the research process.[6]

This book is about architectural interpretation, the ability to find meaning in buildings. This is a skill, like most others, that requires both time and effort to master.

Take, for instance, the two-family house pictured in figure 2. Built in 1906 on Richmond Avenue in Buffalo, New York, the structure is a typical example of lower-middle-class domestic architecture found in urban areas around the country during the early years of the twentieth century. The Richmond Avenue house is an object that has both substance—it is a material reality—and content—it evokes images, ideas, and meanings for its users. But while there can be little doubt that such a building has the potential to communicate critical information about the social and cultural world of its various inhabitants, it nevertheless remains unclear how exactly we might go about deciphering its meaning.[7]

Analyzing and explaining the cultural content of a building is not something you can just *do,* after all, for the Buffalo house is not like a city history book, a building permit, a diary from the Banks family (one of many residents of the property), a letter from a grandparent, or even the federal census. Such documents, because they contain written messages, communicate in a language we readily (if variously) understand. The history might say something about the development of the Richmond Avenue section of Buffalo; the building permit might reveal the date when the house was constructed and even give the name of its builder; the diary might talk about specific events that occurred in the house; the letter might describe how one of the rooms in

Fig. 2. A two-family or double house at 299 Richmond Avenue, Buffalo, New York. Photo by Elizabeth Cromley.

the house was used and list some of its furnishings; and the census would enumerate all the people who lived there at particular times, while also giving their ages, occupations, and places of birth. From these sources we can begin to say something about the history of the house and its occupants.

But what do we learn from the house itself? What does it tell us? "Very little," you might say. It is gray; it is built of wood and covered with horizontal siding; it is two and a half stories high; it has porches on two levels; it seems quite decorative. And depending too on how you feel about such things, the house may seem an attractive or an unattractive creation, a pleasant or a distasteful place in which to live. Beyond such descriptive and subjective observations, though, for the uninitiated there may not be much left to say. Without some kind of technique for interpreting the architectural language of the house, we likely cannot read the physical evidence of the structure as a social or cultural text. We simply need more training.

Learning to read architecture—an ability that centers on a kind of visual and spatially oriented analysis—is not easy. So it comes as no surprise that researchers fall back on the customary written sources when confronting buildings as evidence. They find bits and pieces of information—some mention of an important event that took place here or the names of important people who once occupied the building—that lend significance to the object rather than confronting the physical evidence. We apply the known to the unknown, saying that "the house is significant because it is associated with such and such person or this or that event," but we still have not studied the materiality of the building—its fabric, plan, and stylistic features—for what that may say about human behavior. Vernacular architecture research implies a marriage of sources: oral history, written documents, and the buildings themselves. Still, no matter how much extrinsic data there is, the evidence obtained by studying the physical object lies at the heart of the research.

As might be evident by now, students of vernacular architecture are not on the whole what might be called "library" scholars. If you are interested in studying buildings, particularly those of the more ordinary variety that have not been studied before, the place to begin is with the buildings themselves. "Buildings," Gabrielle Lanier and Bernard Herman tell us at the beginning of their guide to architecture in the Mid-Atlantic region, "are the best teachers of ordinary architecture. Books, drawings, photographs, and written documents are invaluable, but, inevitably, we learn the most about buildings by taking to the field—by looking, evaluating, measuring, questioning, and looking again." Fieldwork—the recording of buildings in situ with measured drawings and photographs—is one of the distinguishing features of vernacular architecture as a field of study (fig. 3).[8]

In some instances architectural data can be assembled in other ways. One can study buildings depicted in literary sources such as pattern books, advice manuals, probate inventories, court records, or even novels. Maps, blueprints, historic photographs, and paintings can also reveal information about vernacular architecture. It may be that buildings important to your study are gone—demolished or fallen down—so that the standing record is incomplete. In such cases you may need to reconstruct the missing pieces from whatever information is available: a footprint on an old fire insur-

Fig. 3. Fieldworker Kathryn Anderson measuring the newel post on the staircase of the Peter Greaves Family House, Ephraim, Utah. Photo by Thomas Carter.

ance map, a description in a diary, or a rare surviving photograph. But whatever your sources, the focus of attention remains on the building.

Sometimes, in studying contemporary buildings, you may find the people who made or used the buildings speaking about how they were used or what they meant. In some cases you may even watch and observe how people behave in various architectural environments. As you move further back in time, however, and the testimonies or actions of users are missing, a well-trained eye for what was built, used, remodeled, or even torn down may be all you have. Reading buildings requires something of a leap of faith: faith in yourself as an objective onlooker and faith in your methodology. At some point you have to decide what it is all about. There are no intrinsic truths but only your own story of what happened. However, if you have done your homework well, if you have systematically built up a reliable body of data, and if you have applied proper theories of analysis, the opportunity is there to discover highly complex meanings in even the simplest of forms.

As you become more familiar with the world of buildings, a set of basic questions emerges to guide your work. In looking again at the Buffalo house on Richmond Avenue, you might ask if the house type was new to the city—that is, does it represent a continuation of older ideas or the introduction of new ones? Is it unique, or are there others like it in the community? How does the arrangement of rooms compare to earlier Buffalo houses? Are there new rooms—and new functions— for the house? Are some rooms finished differently than others? If so, can we deduce the entertaining or "best" rooms from those used by the family on an everyday basis? Has the house been changed through the years? Does the remodeling reflect a basic change in cultural values in the community? Such questions about time, form, context, and ultimately function are necessary to a deciphering of the building's content—that is, to reading it as a historical text.

Studying buildings, then, requires some special training. The basic vernacular architecture research method, however, is hardly revolutionary: it still requires gathering data, ordering and analyzing the data, and interpreting the data. Our chapters generally follow this sequence. First there is a definitional chapter that introduces the community-based conceptual model underlying our approach to vernacular architecture and vernacular architecture studies. The second chapter provides a brief exegesis of the investigatory techniques used in the field documentation of buildings and landscapes. Chapter 3 shows how both field and archival evidence may be organized into a set of analytical frameworks that help illuminate patterns (or the absence of patterns) of behavior. In chapter 4 we give examples of how various practitioners in the discipline have interpreted buildings and landscapes. And in chapter 5 we end by returning to the house on Richmond Avenue for a quick review of how the ideas contained in this book can be applied to a specific example of architecture. Also provided is a bibliographic survey of sources, which, along with the information contained in the footnotes, should help you move into the material on your own.

At this point, studying buildings is starting to sound like a lot of trouble. If the point of our research is to understand human culture, why not just stick to the usual documents? It is a legitimate concern. We would not suggest that the study of buildings is some kind of academic panacea. Vernacular architecture research is not going to replace other kinds of humanistic inquiry. In the right situations, however, it can contribute greatly in addressing many kinds of questions concerning human behavior. Cary Carson, director of research at Colonial Williamsburg and a historian who uses vernacular architecture as evidence, talks about the need to choose your sources well. "Because research is so time-consuming," Carson writes, "historians observe a principle I call the Rule of Least and Best; they achieve a necessary efficiency in their work by gathering the least amount of best information needed to solve their problem."[9] The trick in vernacular architecture studies is to figure out when and under what circumstances buildings and landscapes become the best documents for answering particular kinds of historical questions, since studying them will likely require considerable time and effort. When does the rule of least and best kick in, then, for buildings? Certainly a case-by-case evaluation is warranted; but generally speaking, material culture study is attractive for the following reasons.

First, buildings have an "ethnographic" quality missing from many other kinds of historical documents. Ethnography, as a branch of anthropology, is generally defined as the scientific study of human culture, but the term also refers to an investigative technique by which the researcher is able to observe directly the human behavior being studied, thereby removing, at least theoretically, the chance that the evidence will be tainted by the interpretations of others. Ethnographic research implies, then, immediate contact with the behavior being studied.[10]

Historians, of course, have no such ability, for the people they are interested in learning about are generally dead and gone. It is often said that the past can only be known through its remains, the trick for historians being, then, to find the best kinds of remains to study. Most historians are drawn to written documents from the past because they are, as suggested above, the most easily read. The trouble, however, is that with such records as journals, diaries, notebooks, and histories, no matter how reliable their authors may be, the reader is always left with essentially secondhand or indirect accounts of what happened—the written document stands between us and the actual behavior being written about. At this intermediate stage, a particular person gives his or her own view of what took place, and obviously the action is filtered through that individual's own perceptions, biases, and knowledge. Even the most primary evidence, then, is secondary in that it is at least once—and often many more times— removed from actuality.

In recent years historians such as Rhys Isaac have offered up an "ethnographic" model for doing history in which the historian scans the written record for the recurring actions that betray the workings of culture. "In the documents surviving from the past," Isaac writes, "the social historian can everywhere find traces—occasionally vivid glimpses—of *people doing things.* The searching out of the meanings that such actions

Fig. 4. Around 1820 the Henry Dubois family built a new house in New Paltz, New York. The house was curious in that the front elevation was constructed of red brick and the less visible remaining walls—those to the sides and back—of roughly laid limestone. No family members wrote down the reasons for this particular design solution, nor can an explanation be found in local histories. The fact of the house, however, remains as evidence of human behavior that is directly available to us for interpretation. By looking at the house we might surmise that the Dubois family's finances prohibited building the entire house of brick, which was a prestigious but expensive material. Rather than foregoing the status that brick afforded, they put their money where it would do the most good, on the front, where their good taste and apparent affluence could be seen by all. Photo by Thomas Carter.

contained and conveyed for the participants lies at the heart of the enterprise [that is] ethnographic history."[11] And of course if we are looking for "traces of people doing things," then it is easy to see that one of the main things people did in the past was to build and/or use buildings, and with such objects we do not have to rely on what people said about them. We can, if the buildings have survived, interpret them for ourselves. The architectural historian Camille Wells puts it this way: "historic architecture is one aspect of the past that we can still see, touch, experience . . . and part of what attracts us to old buildings is their insistence on communicating, in some outmoded dialect we do not entirely understand, the energy and purpose, the achievements and hopes, the disappointments and hardships of those who made and used them."[12] In the ways that all kinds of buildings are constructed, in the ways they are styled and decorated, and in the ways they are used and reused (and reused), later observers are able to see the end results of people making actual decisions about how their world will be ordered (fig. 4).

A second area where artifactual evidence is crucial is in recovering the stories of people who left no other kinds of records. As mentioned, archaeologists deal with material culture because there is little if any written documentation for early periods. But even in times of historical record-keeping, most people do not write about themselves and most do little that makes others want to write about them. But everyone makes, or buys, and uses *things,* and in such cases where conventional history methods fail, material culture is what we have to work with. Buildings and assemblages of buildings make excellent sources of information about everyday people and everyday life because they exist in great numbers and are complex enough to shed light on many aspects of human behavior, from attitudes toward the use of space to aesthetic traditions and technological know-how. If we feel that history ought to be an endeavor that includes the widest range of people possible—rich and poor, black and white, ordinary and extraordinary, male and female— then we need to utilize the widest possible range of sources, and buildings are one such source (fig. 5).[13]

Fig. 5. Countless now-nameless immigrants moved through tenements like this one in New York City's Lower East Side neighborhood on their way to the American Dream. The people are gone, but the buildings remain. Photo by Thomas Carter.

A third reason for concentrating on architectural evidence is that buildings often reveal aspects of behavior such as the mundane or the forbidden rarely spoken of in conventional texts. Structures have a way of showing us things about ourselves that we may feel are too mundane to mention but which nevertheless articulate routines essential for our survival. And certainly there are skeletons in the closet—things we do not want to talk about—for example, slavery or the suppression of women's rights. These features are part of what the geographer Pierce Lewis has called our "unwitting autobiography." In the way we create and use architectural space, we say things we would never say in our journals or diaries. There are many taboo topics, such as class differences—rarely talked about in the United States—that become evident in the architectural landscape. The distribution of buildings mirrors the distribution of the population according to economic class and makes such divisions visible not only in the sizes of houses, but also in the way the buildings of the rich and powerful physically dominate the landscape by their location and presence (fig. 6).[14]

Fourth, objects are essential in the study and understanding of the artfulness of a culture. To understand how people bring beauty to their lives, one must study the buildings themselves rather than literature about them. For example, one can learn much about a culture's aesthetic preferences by simply looking at the way construction materials are treated. Wooden surfaces left in a natural state, which appeared in nineteenth-century romantic designs and again in the arts and crafts era, suggest a self-conscious attempt to express a cultural affinity for nature, while a cultural value for the

Fig. 6. The social stratification of late eighteenth-century Providence, Rhode Island, is evident in this 1790 map. The city's wealthy social elite, including merchants, clergy, and government officials, lived in the large houses at the top of the drawing, which were built on College Hill, above the bustling harbor below. "Providence in 1790" by John Fitch. Courtesy The Rhode Island Historical Society.

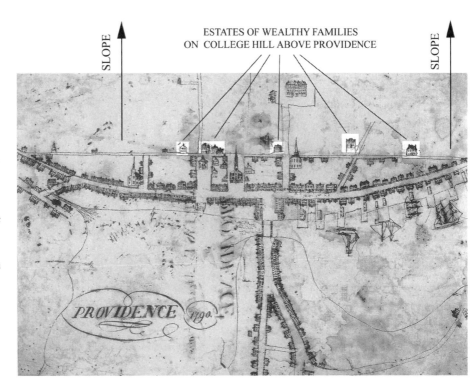

rational and artificial might be expressed in a highly regular and processed finish. Decoration and color are also important cultural indicators. One group's taste might lean toward the embellished baroque style, for instance, while the aesthetic philosophy of another could be driven by asceticism and restraint. A building's appearance is never left to chance, but rather is based on a system of culturally determined ideas of what is considered suitable or beautiful to behold (fig. 7).[15]

Determining history through buildings has its drawbacks, certainly. One has been mentioned already: the time it takes to do fieldwork. Another problem is the uneven rate of survival of buildings. Smaller houses tend not to endure, so the material record may be skewed in favor of the elites, just as the written record is. If we are trying to use buildings to get information about common people in everyday life, we will often be disappointed since much of the evidence from early periods of history is gone. It would be easy, for example, looking at the architectural landscape of New England now, to think that people of the past were better off than they really were, for usually it is the bigger houses that survive. We have to be careful to reconstruct the proper percentages of houses in each economic level in the past and not to take the standing evidence for granted (figs. 8 and 9).[16]

In the end, you will find that the best reason for studying buildings is the potential they hold for helping us in the humanistic endeavor of better understanding who we are and why we have done the things that we have. As both the products of culture and its agents, buildings reflect our cultural values. Once created, they not only become symbolic representations of those values but also serve in their own way to enforce those values actively, making sure that they are adhered to and followed. In this sense, as anthropologists point out, the material world is *reflexive:* architecture, in the words of the social theorist Mark Gottdiener, "possesses the dual characteristics of being both a product of social relations and a producer of social relations."[17]

Fig. 7. Following Old World custom, the interior walls of nineteenth-century German immigrant buildings in the upper Midwest were often covered with brightly colored painted ornamentation. This example is from the best room of a tavern in the community of St. Mary's, Butler Township, Franklin County, Indiana. Photo by Thomas Carter.

Fig. 8. This large center-chimney, hall-parlor house in Wethersfield, Connecticut, is typical of those buildings that have survived all over New England from the late seventeenth century and the first half of the eighteenth century. Photo by Thomas Carter.

Take, for example, a typical classroom (figs. 10 and 11). In both its formal organization and its use, the room reflects a normative approach to the education process. The teacher's space is to the front, facing out toward the students who sit in neat rows of chairs/desks, all bolted to the floor. Everyone has his or her own desk—his or her own space—reflecting the American value of individuality. There is no danger of one student violating another's territory. The whole room is ordered by tripartite symmetry. There are three rows of overhead lights. The blackboard is divided into threes, with the center panel being the most prominent. Only the teacher's podium is off-center, a decision necessitated by the need to use the retractable screen in the center for showing slides. In its form, then, the room adheres to all the conventions proper to educational space in the United States.[18]

Fig. 9. Small New England houses of one or two rooms and dating to the late seventeenth, eighteenth, and early nineteenth centuries are rare today but were numerically predominant during the colonial and early federal periods. These examples have either been demolished or incorporated, as was this one in Lincoln, Rhode Island, into larger, more modern buildings. Photo by Thomas Carter.

Fig. 10. Room 228, Art and Architecture Building, University of Utah, Salt Lake City. Photo by Thomas Carter.

The physical properties of the room, so constructed, ensure that these values are enforced and that those who use the room adhere to them as well. The key feature of the space is that the desks are bolted to the floor so that they cannot be moved. Neither students nor teachers could try new ways of seating or of breaking up the teacher-facing-students format, even if they wanted to. Teachers are forced to remain at the front. Education emanates from front to back, and the room ensures compliance to this format.

There is a great deal to learn about studying buildings for meaning. This book cannot touch on all aspects of vernacular architecture research, but it can make a start. Part of what we want to do here is to introduce and define the field, which is not easy since, like most disciplines, vernacular architecture is a realm of inquiry that is con-

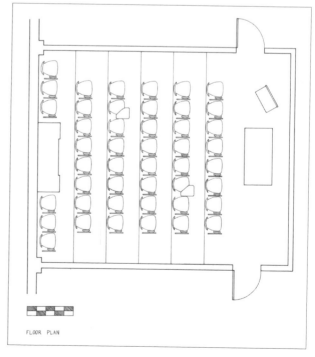

Fig. 11. Floor plan of Room 228, Art and Architecture Building, University of Utah, Salt Lake City. Drawing by Collin Tomb. Used by permission of the Western Regional Architecture Program, University of Utah.

stantly evolving and changing. It incorporates many perspectives, and there are many ideas about what it is. The study of vernacular architecture has been around long enough, however, to have achieved some stability, patterns, and conventions, and our interest here is to highlight some of these commonalities in a way that presents a fairly unified, declarative statement of what the field is all about.

In large part this book contains explanations of research methods, techniques, and theories. The method is not ours, but rather one worked out over the past thirty years by a variety of archaeologists, art historians, architectural historians, cultural geographers, folklorists, social historians, and preservationists, to name a few of the disciplines represented in this truly interdisciplinary field. Our focus is the buildings and landscapes of North America from colonial times to the present, although the approaches presented here could be applied to any region or time period. As a crash course in vernacular architecture studies, *Invitation to Vernacular Architecture* should be useful to a wide range of people—both in and out of the academy—wanting to know more about the material world they inhabit. If we have done our job well, this guidebook should give readers, no matter what their backgrounds, enough familiarity with the varied ways of studying buildings that they can begin to make sense of the architectural matrix that surrounds them.

CHAPTER 1

Definitions

The field of vernacular architecture studies, as we know it today, came into its own largely during the 1970s and early 1980s. Architectural history, born during the late nineteenth century out of an abiding curiosity in classical antiquity, slowly but steadily grew through the first six decades of the twentieth century into a respectable, scholarly discipline.[1] Professors lectured on the great periods of art and architectural development, wrote biographies of famous architects, and generally confined themselves to the study of what were perceived to be the crowning achievements of design, from antiquity to the present. All in all, it was a tidy, comfortable discipline in which everyone knew their place and no one rocked the boat; the grand studied the grand, and all was well in the academy. Beginning in the 1960s, however, as part of the general intellectual turmoil of the period, people began to question many of the assumptions that had driven not just architectural history but also the study of history as a whole. The implications of this upheaval for historians of buildings would be profound.

Whether inspired by Marxist tomes or simply antiwar and antiestablishment sensibilities, the cultural revolution of the Vietnam War era had a decidedly leftist slant, a political inclination that manifested itself in the academy as a wave of unprecedented populism. American historians at the time, like their architectural counterparts, were used to approaching their subjects from the point of view of great men (and we mean men, for women played little part), who were mostly affluent and white, and great events—the main cogs in the wheels of progress around which the past unfolded. But as the young radicals of the 1960s were quick to point out, that was a history that left most people—the working class, the poor, people of color, women—out of the story. Here was a history of a small elite minority and the events in which they participated, and ordinary people and everyday life were effectively ignored. So a new kind of history was called for, and it was called just that, the "new history," or alternatively the "new social history" or even "history from the bottom up," so great was the emphasis on the common person. This history was more inclusive and democratic, more even-handed, and focused on the average and ordinary. The work of scholars in this period revolutionized the writing of history. Other disciplines—including architectural history—were not immune to this intellectual

Fig. 12. Edward Whiteman Family house, Crow Indian Reservation, Big Horn District, Montana. Whiteman made a good living leasing Crow land to white farmers and built this frame cross-wing house around 1920. Photo by Thomas Carter.

Fig. 13. Floor plan of the Edward Whiteman Family house, Crow Indian Reservation, Big Horn District, Montana. Drawing by James Gosney. Used by permission of the Western Regional Architecture Program, University of Utah.

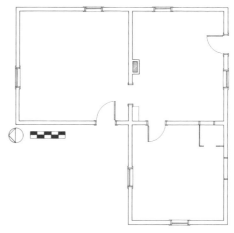

revolt, for they too felt pressure to expand their view to include alternative and minority populations.[2]

For students of architecture, the new history included a broader range of buildings as worthy of study. To be sure, traditional architectural historians still wrote about the leading architects, and the old standards—for example, Monticello, Fallingwater, and 860 Lake Shore Drive—continued to attract adherents in the academy. However, by the 1970s a growing number of scholars found themselves drawn to the commonplace architecture of the masses—the ordinary buildings of ordinary people (figs. 12 and 13).[3]

Their interest developed from the populism of the era, which demanded social responsibility and justice. Jefferson lived comfortably in the big house at Monticello, but where and under what conditions did his slaves live? The department store magnate Edgar Kaufman hired Frank Lloyd Wright to build a cutting-edge vacation house on Bear Run, Pennsylvania, but now historians wanted to know what kind of housing the people who worked in his store had. And while some might applaud the post–World War II steel-and-glass genius of Mies van der Rohe in Chicago, others found popular contemporary ranch houses more significant. Such topics had not been treated before, nor had anyone at the time bothered to reach out to these architectural populations, and it was a shift in perspective that considerably altered the scholarly discourse.

For one thing, connoisseurship, which had dominated the field of architectural history for many years, lost some of its preeminence. Connoisseurship is an approach to analysis in which an expert knowledge of the building fabric, including an understanding of such things as methods of construction, materials and technologies, and decorative finishes, is used to date periods of construction and to evaluate the quality and authenticity of design and craftsmanship. For the new architectural historians, connoisseurship, at least as far as it involved the ability to read the physical evidence of building for meaning, was a legitimate practice, and as we shall see, it is still very much a part of vernacular architecture research. What the new historians of architecture questioned were the connoisseur's goals, which were often solely directed toward developing chronologies or establishing hierarchies of aesthetic merit (proving value in both academic circles and the marketplace). Such an inward-looking agenda, one that focused on the building as an art object, was increasingly unacceptable to a rising generation of populist scholars who saw buildings as stepping-stones to learning about the people who used them. The new architectural historians chose a more socially and culturally directed approach in which, rather than the study of buildings alone, the people and their struggles to fashion social environments through buildings were the objects of research.[4]

The specific methods and techniques for this new approach to architectural history, which in time would crystallize into the vernacular architecture movement of the 1970s and 1980s, came from a variety of scholarly disciplines that included, among others, architecture, folklore, social history, and historic preservation. A full history of the field cannot be recounted here, but it is important to recognize some of the main contributions.[5]

The first serious students of vernacular architecture in the United States were architects who during the 1880s and 1890s engaged in documenting the rapidly disappearing buildings of the colonial generation. Men such as Norman Isham, Albert Brown, and J. Frederick Kelly visited, sketched, and measured important examples of seventeenth- and eighteenth-century New England domestic vernacular architecture. Of great concern to these early fieldworkers was the documentation of the many changes they saw in the historic building fabric. Most colonial-era houses had gone through multiple remodelings, and it was quickly discovered that one could learn a great deal about a building's history from the kind of detailed inspection that went into preparing accurate measured drawings of elevations, plans, framing systems, and finishes, both exterior and interior. Though they could not foresee their influence on a later generation of scholars, these architects nevertheless established, through their systematic recording of extant buildings, a clear precedent for what might be thought of as an archaeological approach to architectural history—one where the building is treated more as an archaeological site in need of excavation and explanation than simply as a singular product of aesthetic invention.[6]

The Society for the Preservation of New England Antiquities (SPNEA), founded in 1906, is one legacy of the pioneering work accomplished by Isham and others. Under the auspices of SPNEA, extensive documentation of colonial-era vernacular buildings continues. Starting in the 1950s, the work of SPNEA director Abbott Lowell Cummings and his students is especially noteworthy. Cummings's early interest in probate inventories as a source for understanding room use in colonial houses paved the way for numerous studies that followed, and his 1979 *Framed Houses of Massachusetts Bay, 1625–1725,* a book that charted the transfer of English building practices to New England, established a standard in the field of vernacular architecture for both meticulous historical research and detailed architectural documentation (fig. 14).[7]

In folklore, the lead was taken by Henry Glassie. As a young graduate student, Glassie had been inspired by the work of American cultural geographers such as Fred Kniffen, scholars who used traditional housing forms to map the movement and distribution of culture groups. Glassie built on this work in a series of increasingly provocative studies, beginning with a historic-geographic survey of material culture traditions that included architecture and moving on to develop a system for explaining the design process behind ordinary objects. He then developed a theoretical model for explaining the effects of modernization on the architectural landscape. Glassie's work, particularly in his eloquent call for the study of common buildings and his concern for meaning in addition to description, provided another important plank in the vernacular architecture academic platform (fig. 15).[8]

Social historians interested in the lives of ordinary Americans also joined the mix. These scholars initially came to the built environment through written sources such as probate inventories, court records, tax rolls, books of real estate transactions, self-improvement manuals, and agricultural journals, but their goal was the same as that of their material culture colleagues. They sought a new perspective on the way the social categories of race, class, and gender influenced the organization of the

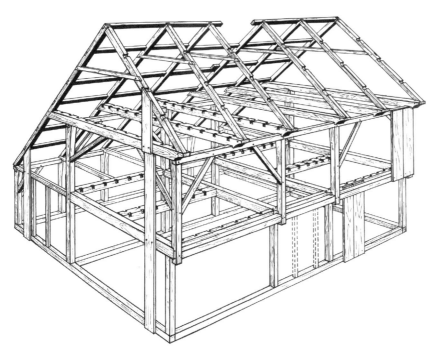

Fig. 14. White-Ellery House illustration by Lawrence A. Sorli. Reprinted by permission of the publisher from *The Framed Houses of Massachusetts Bay, 1625–1725* by Abbott Lowell Cummings, p. 86, Cambridge, Mass.: The Belknap Press of Harvard University Press. Copyright © 1979 by the President and Fellows of Harvard College.

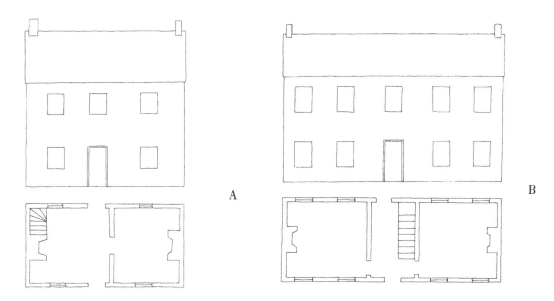

Fig. 15. Schematic representation of the development of the Georgian I-house type: (a) an early two-room—"hall and parlor"—plan; (b) Georgian I-house plan. From Henry Glassie, "Eighteenth-Century Cultural Process in Delaware Valley Folk Building," in *Winterthur Portfolio* 7 (1973): 45. Courtesy of Henry Glassie.

historical landscape, concentrating on household structure, family relationships, reform movements, and urbanization.[9] In time, architectural evidence moved from an ancillary role to a primary role in the work of social historians such as Rhys Isaac, Sally McMurry, Robert Blair St. George, and Richard Bushman.[10]

Another important force in the rise of vernacular architecture studies was the growth of historic preservation as a major player in American architectural history. The passing of the National Historic Preservation Act of 1966 required the federal government actively to monitor publicly funded undertakings to make sure they would not adversely affect the nation's historic and cultural resources. Before an adverse effect could be determined, resources worthy of protection—significant buildings, sites, structures, and landscapes—had to be identified. One of the main contributions of the 1966 act, and the one that perhaps had the most profound impact on the study of American architectural history, was the stipulation that all the states initiate intensive architectural surveys. This work was necessary to determine which properties would be eligible for listing on the National Register of Historic Places, the nation's list of significant properties. With federal monies available through historic preservation grants, state historic preservation offices (SHPOs) hired many surveyors and placed them in communities that had never been looked at before by architectural historians.[11] This work had two consequences.

First, the survey work produced the data for the most important studies of American architecture that had come along in years, studies that, in the tradition of Glassie and Cummings, used careful field documentation to address questions of social and

cultural meanings.[12] Second, because surveyors were pushing into uncharted territory—industrial districts, urban neighborhoods, suburbs of all kinds, as well as the rural
countryside—for the first time students of American architecture had to confront fully
the vast array of ordinary building types. It was an encounter of great value, but one that
also caused some angst, for existing frames of reference and customary descriptive
vocabularies could not be stretched to cover all the new varieties of buildings being discovered in the field.

Surveyors might pick up a reference book such as John Blumenson's *Identifying
American Architecture* or Poppeliers, Chambers, and Schwartz's *What Style Is It?*, but
these books could not solve their problems. The buildings used as examples of American building styles in these books were not the ordinary ones the preservation surveyors were seeing on the streets. Rather, the ones shown in the books were bigger,
grander, and more costly. If a particular style was said to be characterized by a set number of visual characteristics, then the example given had them *all,* implying that only
those buildings with all the requisite features were worthy of being included in
the style category (fig. 16).[13] Compared to the examples in the books, most American buildings were plainer and simpler and seemed to be nondescript and without style
(fig. 17). Since every state's preservation survey form contained a box that had to be
filled out for "style," what was one to do?

Some attempts were made to expand the glossary definitions to cover everyday
examples,[14] but *vernacular* increasingly came to be used as a catch-all term for those
buildings that did not fit into the tight, descriptive stylistic categories. *Vernacular*
became the term used for everything from the plain to the strange and eccentric. The
vernacular designation was inspired in part by a linguistic analogy: since there were
both elite (academic) and common (vernacular) forms of speech, so might there be
elite (academic) and common (vernacular) forms of architecture. Thus, America's
architect-designed buildings increasingly carried the academic or high-style label,
while the remaining majority became labeled as common or vernacular architecture.

Fig. 16. An elaborate
high-style example
of Queen Anne
architecture in
the United States,
c. 1890, Decorah,
Iowa. Photo by
Thomas Carter.

Fig. 17. A smaller vernacular Queen Anne–style house, c. 1890, Bloomington, Indiana. Photo by Thomas Carter.

For many traditional architectural historians, the split was convenient because it made a clear distinction between the academic buildings that they felt were worthy of study and those, the vernacular, that could be ignored. For the new historians, however, those who would in time begin to call themselves vernacular architecture scholars, the term helped identify a missing and valued part of the cultural landscape: the ordinary. Vernacular architecture began to acquire both a degree of comfortable acceptance and emotional appeal. This relationship would be cemented in the creation of a professional academic society, the Vernacular Architecture Forum, established in 1980 to bring together interested scholars and encourage the study of the American built environment in all its diversity.[15]

Defining Vernacular Architecture

So what is *vernacular architecture?* While there will always be disagreement about the boundaries of the category—some people, for instance, follow the English model and equate vernacular architecture with preindustrial or hand-produced folk architecture—for most American practitioners, the term has come to mean both a *type of architecture* and an *approach to architectural studies* that emphasizes the intimate relationship between everyday objects and culture, between ordinary buildings and people. An explanation of the "vernacular" approach to studying buildings fills up most of this book, but there is a need here at the outset to clarify what we mean when we say that vernacular is a type of architecture.[16]

A good place to begin is by drawing the previously mentioned analogy between vernacular architecture and vernacular speech. When applied to language, "vernacular" denotes a way of speaking that is tied to or characteristic of a particular region. Within the United States there are variations of American English that typically are spoken in New England, the upper Midwest, the South, and so on that have strong regional associations. Moving downward in scale, the same holds for smaller localities. We are often able to pinpoint someone's hometown or community by her vocabulary, grammar, and enunciation the vernacular speech she uses.

Another characteristic of the vernacular in language is that it is associated with everyday rather than literary speech. Even though the everyday and literary domains overlap considerably, it is useful nevertheless to point to the differences between the everyday and the formal, the first one more unself-consciously expressive and rising naturally from the circumstances of community life, and the second purposefully following prescriptions established by nonlocal academic norms. Vernacular language is the language most people use, while formal language is reserved for special occasions.

In vernacular speech, then, a strong community identity exists that is manifest in distinctive qualities and results in recognized patterns of everyday language. The same holds for buildings. In vernacular architecture there is a strong community content that is manifest in distinctive qualities and results in recognized patterns of everyday building. The language analogy leads to a simple but effective definition first used by Eric Mercer in his 1975 *English Vernacular Houses:* "vernacular architecture is the common building of a given place and time." In adopting this definition, we follow the lead of Dell Upton and John Michael Vlach, who used it in their 1986 book *Common Places: Readings in American Vernacular Architecture.* Mercer's definition is useful because it centers on the idea that vernacular architecture is simply common architecture—what most people build and what they use.[17]

In dealing with vernacular as common buildings, we must be careful to avoid treating the term *common* in a pejorative way.[18] One definition has a decidedly inferior connotation: "of no special quality, not distinguished by superior or noteworthy character." However, the adjective *common* as used in vernacular architecture studies is actually the first definition in the dictionary: "of or relating to the community as a whole, widespread, prevalent," or more pointedly, "occurring frequently or habitually, widely known." Vernacular architecture is common in the numerical sense, the term *common* referring to quantity, not quality. This interpretation gets us away from value judgments, which are relatively unproductive and highly subjective, and refocuses our attention on the relationship of design to a given community in a specific place.

Vernacular architecture is architecture that is pervasive. It is the architecture most people build and use, comprising buildings that are commonly encountered (fig. 18). And why are certain buildings numerically common? The answer centers on

Fig. 18. Vernacular architecture as a factor of numbers: a row of four-square-type houses, c. 1910, in Staunton, Virginia. Photo by Thomas Carter.

the fact that they are the ones that most closely satisfy people's needs. Architecture in all its forms addresses specific problems of shelter, work, social identity, cultural affiliation, and aesthetic taste. No single building solution meets every demand placed on it; but some cover the essentials better than others, and these are the ones chosen consistently enough by builders and users to show up in great numbers. It is our job as analysts—and the goal of vernacular architecture studies generally—to find out why some buildings became the best solutions. In this sense numbers—the commonality of certain types—become significant, for they tell us that these buildings, rather than being something to ignore, are in fact important to a majority of people and therefore of great significance to historians.[19]

To say that buildings are common also assumes some kind of chronological and geographical boundaries, for things can only be common within a defined context—within a "given time and place," as Mercer puts it. The beauty of such a context-based definition is that it yields a highly flexible model for our work, one that is organized around the particular *kind of community* under investigation rather than a set of specific qualities or characteristics of the buildings themselves. Quite simply, vernacular architecture is building attached to an architectural community, and there are many such communities. Some are small, others large. Some grow; some shrink. Some are rural; some are urban. But inherent in the community concept is the idea of a group of people who inhabit a particular geographical area and who have, through various points in their history, achieved a degree of shared identity in behavior, which includes architecture.

For the purposes of this research guide, vernacular architecture communities may be understood as being local, regional, national, international, or global in size and scale (fig. 19). These categories are not necessarily chronological, though the general trend is unmistakably from local to global. Nor are they mutually exclusive. For example, in our country small, localized architectural communities are most typical of early native

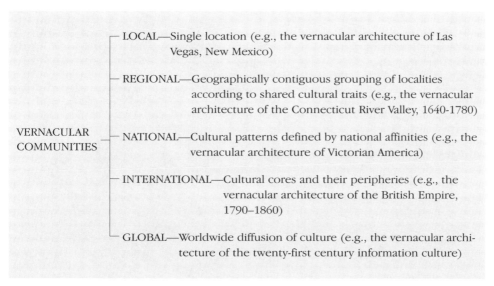

VERNACULAR COMMUNITIES

LOCAL—Single location (e.g., the vernacular architecture of Las Vegas, New Mexico)

REGIONAL—Geographically contiguous grouping of localities according to shared cultural traits (e.g., the vernacular architecture of the Connecticut River Valley, 1640-1780)

NATIONAL—Cultural patterns defined by national affinities (e.g., the vernacular architecture of Victorian America)

INTERNATIONAL—Cultural cores and their peripheries (e.g., the vernacular architecture of the British Empire, 1790–1860)

GLOBAL—Worldwide diffusion of culture (e.g., the vernacular architecture of the twenty-first century information culture)

Fig. 19. Diagram of vernacular communities. Chart by Collin Tomb. Used by permission of the Western Regional Architecture Program, University of Utah.

Fig. 20. Mission Church St. Francis
of Assisi, Rancho de Taos, c. 1780.
Photo by Thomas Carter.

or seventeenth-century European settlements and yet are also found in frontier and immigrant settlements of the nineteenth century and even in suburban cul-de-sacs and inner-city ethnic neighborhoods today. The eighteenth century witnessed the emergence of distinctive regional architectural communities in various sections of the country (fig. 20), but it also saw the incorporation of the colonies along the Atlantic

seaboard into an international community of English market capitalism. After the industrial revolution, faster communication—building designs were published, people traveled, prefabricated building materials become widely available—led to the development of a community of consumers that was national in scope (fig. 21), though local and regional variations on national themes continued. By the beginning of the twentieth century, the distribution of architectural ideas became even wider and some house forms, such as the bungalow, enjoyed global popularity (fig. 22). Today the planet seems to have gotten even smaller, and yet, as the saying goes, there is a

Fig. 21. Houses by mail. Magazines such as *Scientific American* carried designs for houses that inspired buildings all over the country. The example at the bottom, from the November 1891 issue, was interpreted by the builder in the house above, in Westfield, New York. From Daniel D. Reiff, *Houses from Books: Treatises, Pattern Books, and Catalogs in American Architecture, 1738–1950* (University Park: Pennsylvania State Univ. Press, 2000), 123.

Fig. 22. The Bungalow in Gonlbum, New South Wales, Australia. Photo courtesy of Dell Upton.

need to "think globally but act locally." Vernacular architecture has been and will continue to be a mixture of both the immediate and the remote.[20]

The "time-place" or "historic-geographic" context will set the parameters for a vernacular architecture study and predict some of its outcomes. If, for instance, you decide to study the bungalow house type from 1880 to 1900 in California, you will find that it was a rare form and you could study only a few examples. Setting the time boundaries at 1880 to 1900 and the place boundaries in California determines the small number of buildings in the study. Yet by 1920 the bungalow had become the most popular new house form in the state (indeed it was popular globally), so a study beginning at this date might consider hundreds if not thousands of buildings. The buildings that a researcher will examine in the category we call common or vernacular will always depend on the boundaries set for the community under investigation.

Other factors can also generate the identity of a study community. For instance, you could choose to study how architecture helps define social categories based on class, race, ethnicity, or gender. Class distinctions, for example, are everywhere evident in the American landscape, and it may be that a study would look at what historian Cary Carson calls the "politics of space"—how class is worked out architecturally, as a factor of both building size and people's differing access to certain parts of a building or landscape.[21]

Ethnicity—cultural difference formed around race, national heritage, or language—is another factor that shapes the vernacular architecture landscape. Diverse ethnic communities may be found everywhere in North America. Eighteenth-century French settlers in New Orleans and the Mississippi River valley brought familiar building techniques with them from their mother country, executed their buildings with locally available materials, and created architectural manifestations of their French cultural background (fig. 23). Ethnicity remains very much a part of contemporary life. The patterns of African American life, for example, are evident in numerous black neighborhoods throughout the country (fig. 24).[22]

Researchers are increasingly becoming aware of the ways that the landscape is ordered by gender and sexual preference. The predominant users of specific spaces are often sorted according to gender. For example, kitchens in American houses are identified with women, and barns on farmsteads house primarily men's labor. Office buildings in 1900 were the locus of men's work, whereas the contemporary office building may shelter more women employees. There also may be specific areas in cities where gay culture prevails, such as the Castro section in San Francisco. You might, therefore, delimit your study to buildings created for male railroad workers in 1890s Chicago or otherwise use gender to define the community of buildings to investigate.

What is the ideal number of buildings to examine in a vernacular architecture study? This ranges from a single building or a small group of buildings selected from an architectural community to assemblages of buildings and sets of such assemblages. Vernacular architecture scholars make use of a progression of scales in defining the topics for their work. At the smallest scale, you might study an individual building—a house, a barn, a mill, a church, a school, or another architectural object worthy of attention. For example, you could select the house of a mill worker as the object for analysis. You would measure the structure and create a plan showing its room dimensions and relationships, and then analyze its construction techniques and building materials. You could describe its exterior and interior details—from architectural ornament to circulation patterns, heating, and ventilation. At this scale few grand conclusions can be drawn; yet such a study can make a significant contribution to the field by developing a body of data on a given community, one building at a time. Given the time constraints, most vernacular architecture studies focus on a single building, though they are generally conceived within larger research parameters and contexts.[23]

The desire to answer bigger questions leads to a study whose scope is larger than a single building. Groups of architectural elements combine to form architectural communities—linked series of farmsteads or rings of suburbs or

Fig. 23. Creole House, Baton Rouge Parish, Louisiana. Photo courtesy of Dell Upton.

Fig. 24. The Rucher Building, home of the first African-American-owned business in Atlanta. Photo by Dell Upton.

industrial villages and this next step in scale yields useful information. Ensembles of vernacular buildings may be compared with other ensembles to advance the study of vernacular landscapes. We could ask, for example, how the farmsteads of 1850s New England compare to the plantations of 1850s Virginia. How do middle-class 1950s suburban plots outside of Chicago compare to those of the same date in Los Angeles? How were the mills and mill housing of the United States in the 1850s similar or different from the factories and factory housing of the 1950s? How much do railroad suburbs from the later nineteenth century have in common with late twentieth-century automobile suburbs? Buildings and ensembles of buildings gather significance when seen as part of a larger landscape that assemblage of natural features, buildings (high-style and vernacular) and other human interventions taken together. Regional, environmental, and social differences are thrown into relief when sets of buildings are compared.[24]

The term *cultural landscape* has been a handy name for these building ensembles in their settings. By *landscape* we mean the natural environment modified by people to meet their own needs and purposes. Your study of vernacular architecture will benefit from seeing buildings in their larger contexts—that is, seeing wholes. For example, the 1890s house of a miner is better understood when seen in the context of the mines and their equipment but also when juxtaposed to the mine owner's house. The term *cultural landscape* implies ways of observing the order of the landscape as it interacts with social constructions of class, race, gender, and ethnicity. You will find that patterns are much more easily observable if the larger landscape is studied.[25]

Vernacular Design

Any definition of vernacular architecture must at some point address the issues of design and materials. There is a long tradition in this country of viewing the vernacular as handmade, undesigned, ordinary buildings. According to this view, such objects are nothing more than naive responses to purely external, usually environmental, influences and conditions. In terms of materials and construction methods, we would like to move beyond the handmade. For our purposes, vernacular architecture is the common form of building in a given place and time, and therefore must encompass materials both handmade and industrially produced, depending on the particular circumstances. In the contemporary world it is not possible to divide high art from popular art anymore since, as the cultural theorist Victor Burgin writes, "at the levels of production and distribution, all cultural workers today actually or potentially rely on much the same technologies and institutions, and all cultural products are equally subject to commodification."[26] That is, now we all can buy materials at Home Depot (fig. 25).

As for design, our inclination here is to treat all buildings, no matter at what levels of society they occur, as the products of design. Design implies planning the ability to transform ideas about beauty and function into tangible form and this applies equally to all buildings, save perhaps the most expedient. Since constructing a building takes both time and money, nothing gets built unless it is planned, an idea that makes the distinction between academic and vernacular architecture not about design—that one is designed and the other just built—but rather about the nature of that design.

In his germinal treatise, *The Shape of Time: Remarks on the History of Things,* the art historian George Kubler wrote, "man's native inertia is overcome only by desire, and

UTAH'S FIRST PREFABRICATED HOUSE USES UTAH COPPER

Architect's Drawing of Prefabricated Copper House Being Erected At Copperton By Utah Copper Company.

Copper Houses, Inc., an associate of Utah Copper Company, is vigorously developing copper homes as the modern residence of today. Groups of copper houses are now being erected by contractors in several Eastern cities.

Copper houses are attractive, they endure, have low maintenance cost and are moderate in cost. These prefabricated homes may be designed by local architects or by Copper Houses, Inc., and erected by local contractors.

Inquiries are invited from contractors and individuals.

COPPER HOUSES, INCORPORATED
Rust Building
Washington, D. C.

Or, Write or Call

UTAH COPPER COMPANY
Kearns Building — Wasatch 140
Salt Lake City, Utah

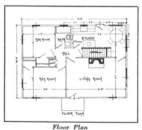

Floor Plan

Basement Plan

ALL HOMES BY COPPER HOUSES, INC., USE UTAH COPPER

Fig. 25. The Kennecott Copper Corporation built the town of Copperton, Utah, for the employees who worked the Bingham Mine near Salt Lake City. At one time the idea was to build the town's houses completely out of copper. From *Utah Magazine* 2 (January 1937): 40.

nothing gets made unless it is desirable." In other words, the vernacular building has not been formed "by accident" or thoughtlessly but rather represents the thought of human beings, and therefore it repays our attention.[27] The modern architect Le Corbusier, in his 1920s book *Towards a New Architecture,* argued that even the earliest, most rudimentary buildings were designed. He described the regulating lines used in laying out even the most primitive community, temple, or house. Primitive man "has had by instinct recourse to right angles—axes, the square, the circle" to make even the earliest hand-built hut.[28] Taken together, these two writers suggest that, rather than differentiating *building* from *architecture* (a term synonymous with "art" or artful building), we need to acknowledge first that all things we make are valued and desired, and second that all buildings are regulated or designed.

But the vernacular design process is different in some ways from design by academically trained architects. One important difference in vernacular design centers on the availability of ideas. Whereas high-style designers exercise the freedom to draw from all possible sources, from the local to the cyber, and aspire to the unique and innovative, in vernacular architecture the range of ideas is more self-contained and limited by either the community of practice or the intended audience and market. Also, the end product would be considered wrong if it fell too far outside the conventional norms of the group, so designs are usually fairly conservative, based on replication rather than invention. This does not mean that there is not change. There is, but new ideas are introduced slowly and melded into older, more comfortable solutions. Constant, small variation within accepted norms is the rule, until the time comes for sweeping changes—the revolutions in the norms of the community where you see a shift from one common kind of behavior to another. For example, southern Massachusetts farmhouses of the eighteenth century used fireplaces for cooking in a large room in the main body of the house. All the community's houses located cooking this way. About 1800 there was a dramatic shift to using cookstoves and adding kitchen ells to backs of houses, reorganizing interior uses and changing the exterior shape. But such dramatic shifts are rarer in vernacular architecture than little changes within an accepted paradigm.[29]

Vernacular design may best be understood as what the French anthropologist Claude Lévi-Strauss called "bricolage"—the assembly of preexisting parts to solve a problem, make a tool, or otherwise create a physical solution. Trained designers formulate anew all elements of the designed product, while *bricoleurs* create a newly designed product out of old parts.[30] Both are designing. The architect Thomas Hubka explained in his article "Just Folks Designing" that vernacular designers go about making design decisions by working from a commonly understood and shared ground of forms and materials that have been tested in a specific community over generations, in contrast to professional architects, for whom originality is an important concern.[31] Yet, like academic designers, vernacular builders make design decisions about space, form, community values, and architectural meaning each time they build (fig. 26).

Sometimes both vernacular design methods and academic methods or "book learning" are applied to designing. In her article on the nineteenth-century North Carolina builder Jacob Holt, Catherine Bishir identified these two levels of designing in Holt's work.[32] Holt built houses following local traditions and using local materials, and at the same time he often reinterpreted architectural ideas that he found in published pattern books. He designed houses that would be both fashionable in their references to stylish publications and serviceable in regional terms. Like high-style buildings, vernacular structures speak about the architectural expression of community traditions and relationships, are ordered by hierarchies of function, and convey both ceremonial and utilitarian meanings.

Once constructed, all buildings then change as they respond to people's changing needs over time. Accounting for the growth and alteration of structures leads vernacular architecture scholars to place the users of buildings in the foreground and to pay attention to the life-span of a building rather than only to its form when first built. It could be said that design happens continuously as people inhabit a building and urge it to meet their needs. Few people can afford to construct new buildings from scratch, but everyone has the opportunity to participate in making a building perform. Making changes in furnishings or in the use of rooms is within everyone's experience. In looking at landscapes, we are concerned in the same way with waves of both building *and* rebuilding. Vernacular architecture scholars have moved away from the connoisseurship model in which change is viewed as distancing the building from the original (and most significant) design, and in the process they have expanded the questions typically asked by architectural historians when they look at buildings. Architecture, from this perspective, becomes a living and changing thing rather than a static work of art.[33]

The term *vernacular architecture* identifies pervasive, commonly built objects and ensembles. Architectural objects in the United States usually described as vernacu-

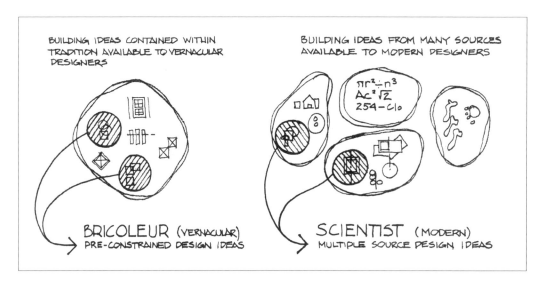

Fig. 26. Diagram by Thomas Hubka contrasting the kinds of ideas available to the *bricoleur* and the modern academic designer. From Thomas Hubka, "Just Folks Designing: Vernacular Designers and the Generation of Form," in *Common Places: Readings in American Vernacular Architecture*, ed. Dell Upton and John Michael Vlach (Athens: Univ. of Georgia Press, 1986), 430. Courtesy of the Association of the Collegiate Schools of Architecture.

Fig. 27. Charnley House, Chicago. Photo by Thomas Carter.

lar examples include log cabins, rural farmhouses, slave quarters, and barns. More recent objects such as Sears-Roebuck house kits, tourist cabins, and grain elevators have been added to the list. In learning to study these kinds of objects, vernacular architecture scholars have developed useful methods that might be applied more widely. That is, there is a set of "vernacular questions" that can be usefully applied to all built works. If you were studying a mansion designed by an elite architect, you would learn more about the work if you investigated who lived or worked in the structure, what regional inflections it bears, or what alterations it has sustained in response to the ongoing lives it shelters. For example, the 1895 Charnley House (figs. 27 and 28) in Chicago, designed by the famous American architects Louis Sullivan and Frank Lloyd Wright, is a high-style work of architecture. Its facade has often been published to convey aspects of Sullivan's and Wright's Chicago style. Yet much more understanding of this work of architecture is to be gained by asking vernacular questions about the house: Who lived there? How did they use the several rooms of the house? Were the array of

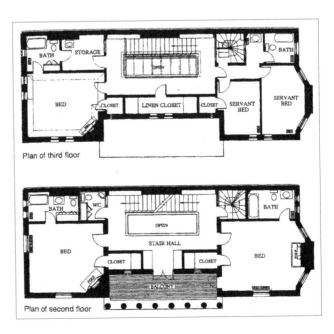

Fig. 28. Plan of the Charnley House. Courtesy of John Eifler Associates.

room functions and adjacencies typical for the Charnleys' class and neighborhood? How was the house changed and adapted to the needs of subsequent owners? In short, vernacular architecture studies have made available methods of inquiry that all scholars of architecture can use as tools to investigate both elite architectures and vernacular environments.[34]

Now you know what vernacular architecture is: as a set of objects, the common buildings of a given place and time; as ensembles of buildings or vernacular landscapes, the products of a particular architectural community; as vernacular architecture studies, an approach to studying buildings as cultural manifestations. These concepts provide a useful entrance to the world of ordinary buildings and will constantly resurface as analysis begins and interpretations unfold.

CHAPTER 2

Architectural Investigations

Looking back on the great amount of time and effort needed to assemble the data for his book *Folk Housing in Middle Virginia,* Henry Glassie observed that "it would not have been necessary to study all of the area's dwellings; only *one* could have been chosen so long as it was the *right one.*"[1] However, Glassie realized that it is necessary to study all the buildings, or at least a good sampling of them, because knowing which one is the right one—the one example that contains all the essential elements of a particular architectural community—is impossible at the outset. In beginning a study, you cannot know what you will find; hindsight alone yields such wisdom. You should come prepared with the best method possible for gathering data and the time needed to carry it out. The first is easier than the second, for the principal commitment in vernacular architecture research is time—time spent gathering, documenting, and analyzing the raw architectural data on which a study will be constructed.

In choosing to study numerically common architecture, one generally ends up looking at a lot of examples rather than sticking to a single building. The actual boundaries and scope of a research topic will always depend on the kind of community under investigation and the type of questions you are asking. It is true too that in starting out, many students will focus on studying one building well, rather than taking on a lengthy and involved project. Whether you are conducting a large comprehensive study or an investigation limited to one or two examples, however, an awareness of numbers is important, for a task in vernacular architecture studies is to look for representative examples that can speak for broad segments of the population. The methodology outlined here is directed toward finding and studying representative buildings. When studying individual buildings, researchers should attempt to see these structures within their larger context, as being representative of larger architectural communities. Start by taking small steps, but know that each step counts since every bit of documentation contributes to knowledge about everyday building in the United States.

Ideally, the research process begins with the framing of a problem or question for which the research will provide an answer. Some questions are narrow and concrete: for example, what kinds of corner-notching did Finnish immigrants use on their log buildings in northwest Wisconsin? Other problems may be broadly stated, having to do with general patterns of behavior in a particular community. Such a study, for example, may simply start out as an attempt to use architecture to help understand how social networks are constructed and maintained in downtown Manhattan in New York City. It is a good idea to have a research goal, though like the number of buildings needed in your research, the range of interpretive implications of the project will probably only be known when you are deeply immersed in the topic. Do not be afraid of the unknown; the best ideas often emerge naturally during the journey of discovery.

Once a research problem has been identified and a historic-geographic focus determined, it is then time to start gathering the architectural evidence. Generally, we suggest four steps in this work. First is the preliminary research done before you begin the main study. The second step is a field-reconnaissance survey of properties and/or landscape features and an initial inventory of published, archival, and other sources. These activities generate the primary data for the research and allow decisions to be made about what needs to be studied in greater detail. The third step is generating the architectural documentation of representative buildings and features with photographs, measured drawings, and interpretive diagrams. The fourth step entails conducting extensive archival and ethnographic research to find out as much as possible about the individual sites under scrutiny so that more general patterns of behavior become evident. Architectural and archival documentation often occur simultaneously: most often you are collecting historical data while doing fieldwork. For reasons of organization, however, we treat the recording of buildings first, in this chapter, and then shift to the library, archival, and oral sources in chapter 3.

Preliminary Research

Before field and archival research begins, a good working knowledge of the study area, its people, its history, and the kinds of architectural and landscape resources likely to be encountered there should be developed. Since the research experience moves from the known to the unknown, the more one has looked at culturally specific buildings, the more comparatively sophisticated the initial analysis will be. Whatever your skill level, however, at this point an introductory visit to the study site is useful. Familiarizing yourself with the place—learning the lay of the land, so to speak—comes in handy in several ways: not only will you know better the kinds of buildings likely to be found, but also you will be able to ask better questions of both the architectural data and the people with whom you meet and talk. Traversing the area to see what the various architectural resources are, where the clustering of historic buildings occurs, and what parts of the community stand out as potentially rich sources of information can come in handy. Sometimes the buildings you expected to find are just not there, or are not found in the numbers or condition imagined. *Know before you go* is a useful adage for doing architectural fieldwork.

During the preliminary stage of the research, one uses mostly *secondary sources.* Secondary materials are technically secondhand accounts of or commentaries on the actual events or objects under consideration. These materials differ substantively from *primary sources,* which, as the name implies, center on the record supplied by the actors themselves in their own words and through their own actions (remember that buildings are primary sources of historical information since they are the direct results of human actions). Examples of secondary sources are published histories, which are often based on primary evidence but are authors' interpretations or impressions of people and events.[2]

   Maps are crucial at this stage of the work. Useful maps will range in scale from those covering the largest amount of terrain to the smallest and most detailed in scale. Different kinds of maps will be available for different kinds of research topics, for different parts of the country, and for different chronological periods. Make sure to check all possible sources for maps that relate to your particular study community. United States Geological Survey (USGS) maps are good for the reconnaissance surveys of rural areas since they not only give you topographic features and elevation contours but also include towns, roads, and individual properties (fig. 29). County atlases, which often contain illustrations and locations of buildings, are also recommended for surveying rural areas.[3] Plat maps, which record the division of land parcels, work well for surveying both large and small urban locations (fig. 30).

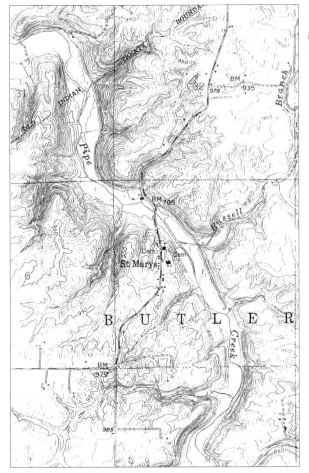

Fig. 29. (left) USGS map for the St. Mary's District of Butler Township, Franklin County, Indiana. The small rectangular dots represent buildings, black for houses and open for outbuildings and abandoned structures, making these maps ideal for reconnaissance-level survey work.

Fig. 30. (above) City plat map showing original urban lots in the "Over the Rhine" district, located north of the first city plat of Cincinnati, Ohio, 1855. Courtesy of Brenda Case Scheer.

Historic maps, too, should be consulted whenever possible. Not only will they reveal the older parts of a community, but some of them from different dates can also provide a chronological portrait of your study area, showing how it has changed or not changed through time. Of particular value in researching nineteenth- and twentieth-century urban buildings are the Sanborn fire insurance maps. Sanborn maps were prepared for fire insurance companies and other underwriters. They are available for most sizable American towns and cities and are good reference works because they show not only the configuration of streets but also the footprints of all the buildings. Even better, the Sanborns are color-coded showing building materials for all structures, which are further identified by height and use. Sanborn maps were regularly updated, so it is possible to compare sheets from different years and get approximate dates for when certain buildings and kinds of neighborhoods (industrial, commercial, working class—indicated by the density of housing) show up (figs. 31 and 32).[4]

The final step in the preliminary phase of the research is developing a work plan. How do you intend to go about the study? Where and when will you begin? What is the projected ending date? How many buildings will be included? Are appointments

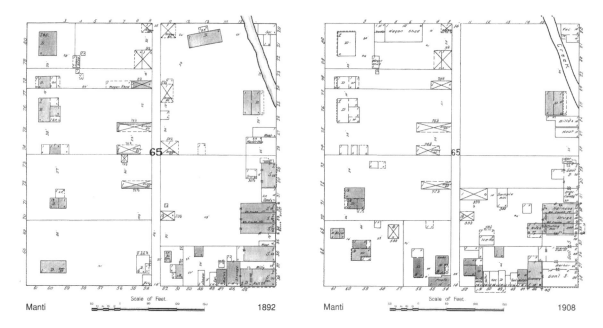

Figs. 31 and 32. For researching nineteenth- and early twentieth-century topics, the Sanborn fire insurance maps are particularly useful. Created as a documentary record for insurance purposes, the Sanborn maps cover the core areas of many American cities and towns. They were begun in the 1870s and 1880s and were updated at regular intervals into the 1950s and in some cases into the present. The Sanborn maps provide good information about building use (building functions are indicated), materials (the buildings are color-coded by construction material: blue is stone, red is brick, yellow is frame), height, and orientation. Construction and demolition dates of individual properties can be ascertained by looking through a series of the maps and noting when certain buildings appear and disappear, as they do in these two Sanborn maps from Manti, Sanpete County, Utah. The left map is from 1892, and the right one is from 1908. Note the appearance of new buildings during this time span.

with building owners and local informants necessary? What materials will be needed (see checklist below)? These are just a few of the questions you should ask in drawing up a plan for the project, but they are questions you should to be thinking about in some detail, especially if a grant application is needed to fund the research.

Reconnaissance Survey

A student, knowing the importance of field documentation in vernacular architecture studies, once asked, "I know I'm supposed to go out and measure buildings, but how do I know which ones to measure?" This is a legitimate question. How *do* we know which buildings warrant intensive recording and investigation—which buildings, that is, are the *right ones* to study? The ability to make good, informed choices about which buildings to focus attention on comes from knowing the material in such a way that significant aspects of the landscape emerge naturally as part of the research process. Impressionistic judgments and subjective attractions should be avoided. Also, expect to make mistakes: the road to understanding a new community of buildings is never straight.[5]

Knowing which buildings to document intensively derives from knowing well the whole. We have found that it is easy to be drawn to those architectural examples that seem somehow exceptional: the log house with the cantilevered roof, the small brick cottage with the onion-dome turret, or the store with the fancy cast-iron facade. While such structures may be important in the overall study, as we indicate below, they should not dominate the work. Be advised, too, that buildings with friendly owners are attractive and make your work easier, but they make for a poor scientific sampling. Informed choices are based on an analysis of the reconnaissance survey data; remember that the goal is to identify *representative* examples, buildings that speak for the larger architectural population.

In vernacular architecture studies, our eyes are turned naturally toward the typical. But this does not mean that only the most routinely encountered structures are surveyed. In regard to what you should look for, several rules apply. First, the typical is often made more meaningful when compared to the atypical, so it is a good idea to locate and identify academically designed or otherwise exceptional buildings and features so that you may return to these examples for further study and documentation. Buildings that for one reason or another do not seem to fit the normative mold are crucial in seeing the varieties of design decision-making in a community. Second, the buildings and landscapes of the upper classes often reveal patterns of social distribution and differentiation visible in the larger landscape. A mansion, for example, might seem from the outside just another high-style artifact and yet when dissected becomes a demonstration of widely held attitudes toward male and female space, and toward the served and their servants. Common people also inhabit and use uncommon spaces. Third, it is often said that the best vernacular architecture studies are those that look at *all* the kinds of buildings within the community under investigation—big and little, rich and poor—to see how they work together within the social and cultural environment in which they are found.[6]

The reconnaissance survey involves briefly though systematically identifying the buildings found in the study community. Ideally a survey will include all the buildings found within your selected geographic and chronological boundaries. More likely, however, you will probably be surveying representative samples within the whole. An example would be a study of the vernacular architecture of cattle ranching in the Great Basin region of western Utah, northern Nevada, eastern California, and southern Oregon and Idaho. As a study community, the Great Basin offers an excellent opportunity to see how the human landscape in that part of the West was adapted to raising cattle on horseback. However, the place is just too vast to be effectively surveyed in its entirety—such work would take years. Historical research strongly suggests that the northeastern corner of Nevada, settled early and home to the requisite architectural elements of ranch culture (horse barns, bunkhouses, cookhouses, and the like), can be viewed as a representative area within the larger community. Furthermore, within this district the ranch architecture found in four principal drainages—the Thousand Springs, Mary's, North Fork, and Owyhee River valleys—can be considered indicative of the larger building tradition (fig. 33). In this way, by continually narrowing the focus of the investigation, whether it is in rural Nevada or central Manhattan, the survey process is streamlined so that it becomes manageable.

In cases when specific building types—say churches or factories or grain elevators or suburban ranch houses— are being studied, then the survey can either include all examples within a set study area or, again, you can concentrate on developing a representative sample. Surveying buildings associated with specific social and ethnic groups follows a similar course; examples are identified and mapped. If you are looking at buildings found in the architec-

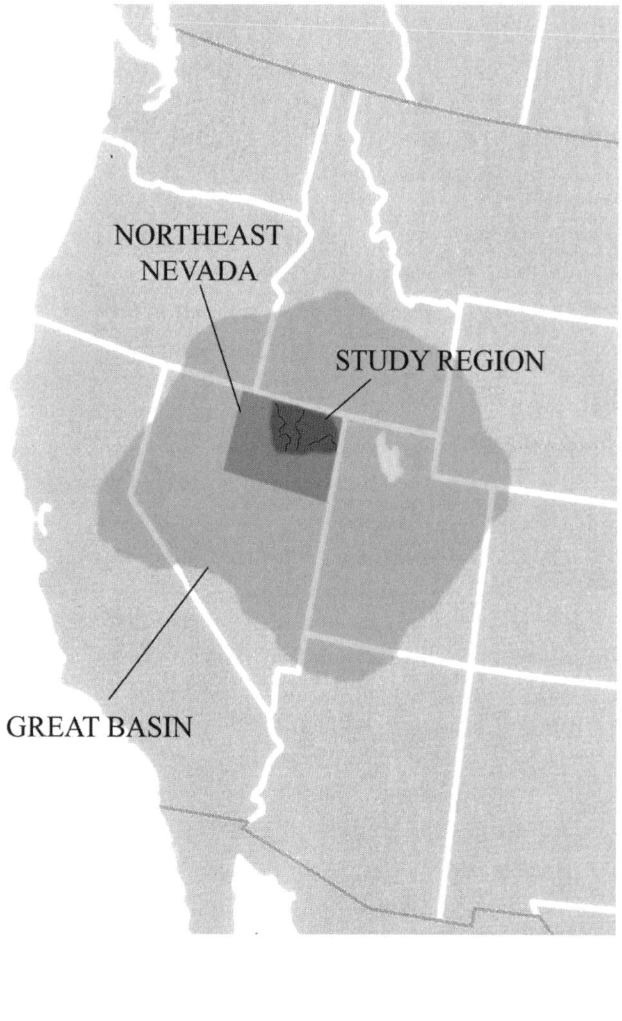

Fig. 33. Example of a representative study area in Nevada. The lightly shaded area indicates the general extent of the Great Basin cattle ranching industry. The northeastern corner of Elko County, considered by many to be the heartland of the region, is denoted by medium shading, while the Thousand Springs, Mary's, North Fork, and Owyhee River valleys, the study area, is located in the center, in the darkest section. Schematic map by Collin Tomb. Used by permission of the Western Regional Architecture Program, University of Utah.

tural literature, your efforts amount to much the same thing. You move through the books or the archive holdings as you would an actual landscape, compiling general information about the various examples that can be used in later discussions of intent and meaning.

Good reconnaissance surveys are based on several activities. The first involves mapping the surveyed sites. Placing the data geographically is important on a practical level so that everyone can know where your evidence is located, but it becomes crucial in later stages of analysis when you start looking for patterns of behavior. As we have already indicated, it is important to choose the map that is right for the kind of survey—rural or urban, local or global—you are conducting. Remember, the goal here is to produce a spatial representation of your data that will be of great value as you begin the process of historical and cultural analysis.

There are several ways to set up survey maps. We have found that it is best to think large. The 18" by 24" sheet size works well because it fits on a large clipboard but is manageable enough to be used in the field or inside a vehicle. Existing maps of all kinds can be enlarged to this size so that enough room will be available to fit the numbers or whatever other symbols you use to plot the surveyed examples. At this scale, too, your markings will be large enough to read easily. When using numbers to identify your sample, it is wise to develop an open-ended system in case a building is missed and must be added later (fig. 34).

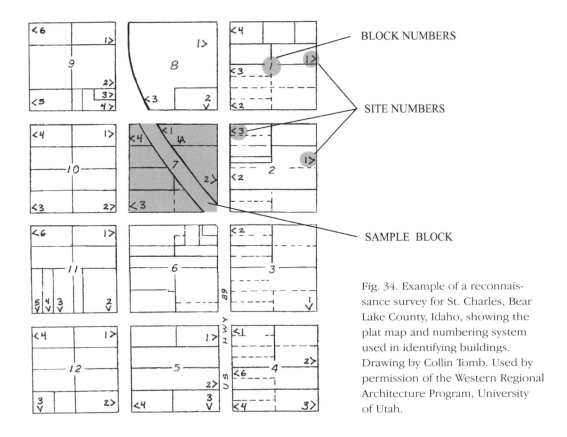

Fig. 34. Example of a reconnaissance survey for St. Charles, Bear Lake County, Idaho, showing the plat map and numbering system used in identifying buildings. Drawing by Collin Tomb. Used by permission of the Western Regional Architecture Program, University of Utah.

A second step in the survey involves briefly describing each building, site, or feature. These short depictions, referring to some aspects of the buildings' form or appearance, are used to identify what is being surveyed so that as the analysis proceeds you will be able to organize the assembled data into meaningful categories. For identification purposes, a working knowledge of the basic building types found in the study area is necessary. You cannot, at this early point in your research, know everything about the building stock under investigation. However, some descriptive

WESTERN REGIONAL ARCHITECTURE PROGRAM
SURVEY FORM

LOCATION (CITY, AREA, ETC):	ST. CHARLES								

COUNTY: BEAR LAKE		STATE: IDAHO					SURVEY DATE: 7/19/82		

SITE NUMBER	APPROX. DATE	BUILDING TYPE	PLAN / TYPE	HEIGHT	MATERIALS	ROOF	OUTBUILDING	ADDRESS / LOCATION	NOTES
1	1900	HS	CW	1	FR	GA	YES	PLAT A BLOCK 18	CROSS-WING
1A	1880	GR	—	1	LOG	GA	NO	"	LOG GRANARY WITH CANTILEVERED FRONT OVERHANG
2	1880	HS	HP	1½	FR	GA	NO	"	HALL-PARLOR/WOOD SIDING
3	1920	HS	BG	1	BR	HIP	NO	"	BRICK BUNGALOW
4	1910	CM	1PT	1	FR	GA	NO	"	1-PART COMMERCIAL BLOCK

Fig. 35. Form that would accompany the map in figure 34, showing the site numbers, descriptive terminologies, and place for notes. Drawing by Collin Tomb. Used by permission of the Western Regional Architecture Program, University of Utah.

terminology is available or can be developed for identifying the examples you have enumerated on your map.

Within a given time and place, a limited number of building types will likely be found, and it may be that your data fall conveniently into these preexisting categories—for instance, a factory, a church, one- or two-part commercial blocks, cross-wing houses, or bungalows. An excellent reference for identifying commercial buildings is Richard Longstreth's *Buildings of Main Street: A Guide to American Commercial Architecture*. A good source for early house and barn types is Henry Glassie's *Pattern in the Material Folk Culture of the Eastern Untied States,* while Lee and Virginia McAlester's *Field Guide to American Houses* and Carole Rifkind's *Field Guide to American Architecture* are good general references for later periods.[7] A partial listing of local and regional architectural guidebooks appears in the checklist of sources at the end of this handbook. In some instances, however, when you are traveling in totally uncharted territory, general descriptions—listing the number of stories, the basic building shape, the type of roof, the construction material—will have to suffice (fig. 35).

Surveys vary with intent. Some research is about houses, so houses are inventoried; other studies look at factories, so these buildings are counted and mapped. Increasingly, students of vernacular architecture are finding themselves looking not only at buildings but also at the larger contexts within which these buildings reside. We have called this larger contextual frame a cultural landscape, an entity that includes a wide range of material features, depending on the nature of life and production in the community. In rural areas a cultural landscape might include fields and pastures, irrigation systems, the layout of the farm, and outbuildings such as barns, corncribs, granaries, and chicken coops. In suburban situations the landscape might be dominated by houses, schools, and shopping centers but enriched by a network of garages, front- and backyard arrangements, fences, decorative plantings, and lawns. Urban cultural landscapes similarly would include a range of features, from the layout of the streets and blocks, to residential and commercial buildings, to neighborhood gathering places, to sidewalks and gutters, to parks and other places of recreation, and even the corner newsstand.

A final note: not all buildings can readily be identified from the outside. During the reconnaissance survey there will be some structures that fall outside existing typologies and deserve a deeper look. Discovering what is going on inside the building may mean getting out of your car and knocking on the door, but it is a worthwhile endeavor if you are interested in picking up the various nuances of the architectural corpus under investigation.

Architectural Documentation

The reconnaissance survey is only the beginning of your investigative work, for the initial survey is primarily intended to identify those buildings and features you will go back to and study in great depth, both architecturally and historically. The mapping of properties that occurs during the inventory process starts to reveal some notable trends: for instance, the big houses are usually found in one particular part of town, with smaller residences often grouped together around a factory. And while it is difficult at this point not to start speculating on what it all means, the best policy is to be patient and concentrate on the work now at hand, which involves intensive-level documentation. The detailed recording of specific buildings and landscape features with photographs and measured drawings is vitally important, for as architectural historian Edward Chappell reminds us, "a relatively limited number of buildings well recorded and analyzed can be more useful than volumes of photos and sketchy descriptions of hundreds of examples."[8]

The first task in the intensive-level stage of investigation is determining which examples will receive more attention. The reconnaissance survey will yield buildings that can be sorted into general categories—by style or type or other relevant qualities—that reflect the main kinds of buildings found in the study community. Some categories may contain many examples, others perhaps only a handful, but from these clusters of similar objects you will choose your representative sample. Ideally, a random selection is taken, say of 5 or 10 percent of the total number surveyed. By maintaining objectivity in this process, you can be relatively certain that your sample is as unbiased as possible.

Several categories of buildings deserve special consideration. There will be some examples that, because of their well-preserved condition, you will definitely want to study because they reveal so much about a particular building tradition. Keep in mind, however, that remodelings and alterations are also part of any architectural history. Do not confine yourself to the pristine, however attractive, and beware of restorations. Sometimes what seems to be an unaltered house is simply a reconstruction of what the owner thought the house may have looked like, or even what they thought the house should have looked like. A critical eye is needed in such circumstances, particularly in areas of the country where historic preservation has been practiced for a long time.

A second consideration in selecting buildings to study centers on what the historian Ronald Brunskill calls the "vernacular threshold." Brunskill's experience researching rural structures in the British Isles suggests that, under normal conditions, "one finds that the many surviving buildings provide a continuous thread [into the past] until a point in time when suddenly all evidence in the form of surviving buildings comes to a stop." Brunskill refers to the point of total disappearance of a particular building type as the "vernacular threshold." The disappearance of a type of building at that threshold varies according to the size of the structure. He writes: "In any locality [the threshold] tends to curve with an ever increasing gradient; examples high on the social scale surviving from an early period, from the middle of the social scale being more recent and from the bottom of the social scale being more recent still." Therefore, concentrating on the few small buildings that hover near the threshold is advised, since such attention is one way to correct for the bias inherent in the uneven ratios (from rich to poor) of surviving buildings.[9]

Another controlling (and sometimes limiting) factor in the documentation process involves finding out which buildings you will have access to, for gaining entrance into houses and other buildings is not always easy, especially in these strange times. Once you have explained the project, presented some credentials (identification and business cards work well), and taken the time to talk with them for a while, most owners are willing to let you crawl through, over, and around their buildings to take measurements and photographs. In some cases, however, coaxing is required. Making contacts in the study area in order to develop a network of people who know you and who can vouch for your good intentions is important. Get in touch with the local newspapers and other media outlets and have them run a story on your project; you will be surprised how fast word gets around. Someone once compared architecture fieldwork to selling vacuum cleaners. The door opens and you have about a minute or two to sell yourself and your work. Being prepared always helps. Have the equipment you need and know how to use it so that when you do have the chance to measure and photograph, you will be ready to work quickly and efficiently. Items of field equipment you are likely to need include the following:

- a large 22" x 28" drawing board
- a supply of 18" x 24" archival-grade graph paper (grid size variable)
- drafting tape to secure the paper to the board
- a mechanical pencil (or the equivalent, and avoid soft leads that smear)
- an eraser or two (since you are bound to make mistakes)
- 20' or 25' wide-blade measuring tape for interior and vertical dimensions
- 50' or 100' measuring tape for longer dimensions
- a strong flashlight (with new batteries)
- access to a ladder
- a 27' measuring pole (surveyors use them to measure the heights of bridges)
- a plumb bob for determining a vertical datum line
- a hand or line level and string for determining a horizontal datum line
- hammer and tacks for setting horizontal datum string
- shoes with thick soles (it is hard to work with a nail through your foot)
- sunscreen and insect repellant
- layering system of clothing (including a hat)

Taking Photographs

Photography in the study of vernacular architecture is essential. Good images are not only needed for publications and presentations but also, when you get back to the office or studio, are important reminders of what you saw. This is not the place to go into great detail about taking pictures. The best advice is to take a photography course or get one of the standard books on the subject, such as Jeff Dean's *Architectural Photography*.[10] The world of photography has changed rapidly, and many researchers now use digital cameras, which yield high-quality images that can be downloaded directly onto a computer and printed easily on regular paper. Digital cameras can also accommodate a variety of wide-angle and telephoto lenses. Some still prefer large-format or 35 mm, single-lens reflex (SLR) cameras with lenses of various sizes: 24–28 mm for interiors and landscapes, 35–50 mm for standard exterior elevations and details, and 85–135 mm for long-distance shots. Several companies make parallax-correcting (PC) lenses, which make the parallel edges of buildings remain parallel in the photograph.

Black-and-white film, because of its high resolution and archival durability, remains the industry standard for both archival documentation and publication, so you might want to have one camera loaded with this kind of film. Power-point techniques using digital images have become popular. Color slides are still used in making presentations. Color prints are generally confined to use as mnemonic devices when drawing up field measurements. Faster film speeds (200 and 400 ASA) are good for working in reduced light situations, while the slower ones (25, 64, and 100 ASA) are best for bright light.

There are several things to think about as you take your photos. First, as you compose your shots, always have in mind what it is you are trying to show and proceed accordingly. Sometimes you need to show a single building, sometimes a construction detail, and sometimes an entire architectural landscape. Second, keep the sun either behind you or to the side to avoid backlighting your subject—having too much light behind your building throws the front into shadow. Third, for interiors bring along a tripod, a flash unit (and the ability to use it), and even some extra lights, which are advisable when things get really dark. And last but not least, with a conventional camera be sure to take photos using multiple lighting exposures (called "bracketing" in the trade) and from a wide range of angles and distances. Compared with the costs in time and gas to get into the field to take your photos, film is cheap, so take some extra shots.

Measured Drawings

Drawing a building—sketching it and trying to figure out how it is laid out, what went into constructing it, and how it may have evolved over time—is a key element in vernacular architecture research. While it is often said that a picture can be worth a thousand words, one good drawing can be worth a thousand photos. Drawings illuminate significant aspects of a building, including its interior arrangement, its "bones" (or skeleton), and its many alterations, which are hidden in conventional photos. They also have the ability to remove extraneous information and center attention directly on the object under investigation (figs. 36 and 37).[11]

Preparing an architectural drawing is a two-step process: first, make a field sketch that records the measurements of a building and its various parts; and second, turn these measured sketches into scaled drawings, either in pencil or ink or on the computer. There are too many techniques and tricks that go into preparing a set of measured architectural drawings for us to explore them all here.[12] We can, however, provide an outline of some of the things you will need to know to get started, particularly how to conduct the in situ field recording of a building. It helps, of course, to have some artistic talent, but if you can't draw, don't worry. Some basic drafting skills, coupled with an ability to use a straight-edge or computer-assisted design (CAD) program (such as AutoCad®), are sufficient to produce a high-quality product.

Figs. 36 and 37. Photograph and section drawing of a food processing shed built and used by the John and Yolanda Bruno family in Helper, Carbon County, Utah. These images demonstrate the effectiveness of the drawing in highlighting both the function and significance of the structure. Photo by Thomas Carter; drawing by Bea Bergold. Used by permission of the Western Regional Architecture Program, University of Utah.

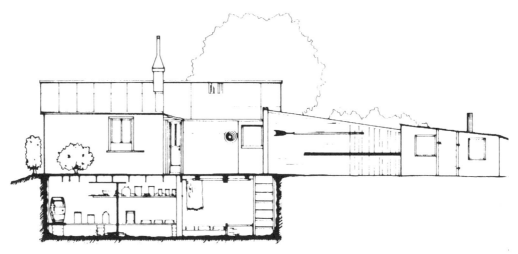

The main kinds of drawings you will be preparing include site plans, which show a building within its immediate surroundings; floor plans, which document the spatial divisions and dimensions of a building; elevation drawings, which may be either of the front, side, or rear of the building, or of interior walls and other features such as staircases, mantels, or built-in cabinets; construction elevations showing building techniques; and section drawings, which represent the building as it would appear if it were cut either by a transverse or a longitudinal plane, so that its internal structure—the framing techniques, particular joinery details, and spatial volumes—is revealed. The same representational techniques used for drawing buildings may also be applied to cultural landscapes (fig. 38), the difference being one of scale rather than orientation.

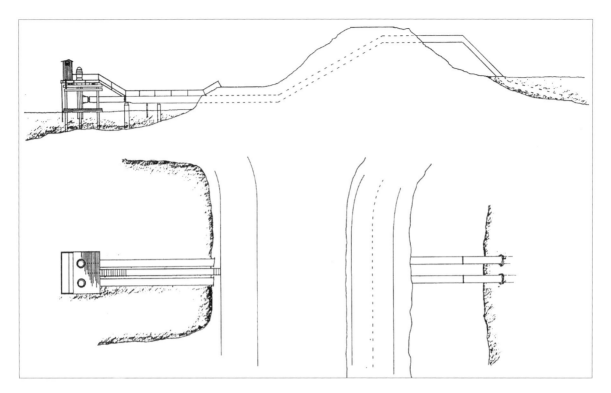

Fig. 38. This cultural landscape drawing depicts, in section and plan, a water pumping station on the upper Sacramento River, California. Drawing by Robert Fabri. Used by permission of the Western Regional Architecture Program, University of Utah.

No matter what you choose to draw, remember that because this process takes time, you will want to direct your drawing efforts to those aspects of the building or landscape that cannot be effectively illustrated through some other means, particularly photography. Exterior elevations, for instance, may be more easily recorded with your camera (unless obscured by foliage), while interior features such as methods of construction and use of space are often more understandable when highlighted through the drawing process.

Recording a Building

Let us say that you have chosen to study the vernacular architecture of German immigrants in the upper Midwest during the middle years of the nineteenth century. After some preliminary sleuthing—including drive-through visits of several potential study areas—you find an ideal location. The area along the Indiana-Ohio border just north of Cincinnati was one of the main destinations for farm families coming from northwestern Germany during the 1830s and 1840s, and many buildings from the settlement period endure here, making it an excellent place to see how immigrant building practices were adapted to the American countryside.

Your work begins with a systematic reconnaissance survey of the study area. Driving the local roads, you identify about 150 buildings and sites that date to the period under investigation. Of these, you decide to document a representative sample—say about 25 to 30 buildings chosen because they reflect the general diversity of the surveyed data. A house in the town of Oldenburg, Indiana, is the first one you will stop to measure (fig. 39). Title research (described in the next chapter) shows that the house was built for the Brink family but that later occupants were the Wagners. It is locally called the Wagner house or the "convent house" because it is located just down the street from the Holy Family Catholic Church, the principal church in the region.

Documentation starts with a thorough visual inspection of the one-and-one-half-story frame house with a lean-to extension to the rear. The small, classically inspired half-windows on the upper front elevation, you note, are part of the stylistic vocabulary of the community found on many examples. Because it is vacant and showing signs of decay, you are able to see normally hidden construction features under some of the exterior clapboards and behind the plaster that is starting to peel from the interior walls. A close look reveals that the entire building is of timber-frame construction, which means that it was built using hand-hewn timbers secured with mortise-and-tenon joinery to form a substantial frame skeleton to which siding and plaster were applied. Furthermore, you can see that the house was probably built in two stages. In the east front room the interstices between the vertical posts are infilled with willow branches packed with mud, a technique called wattle and daub. This technique is characteristic of the earliest period of settlement in the area. The remaining rooms to the west and north are also timber frame but different. Here the infill consists of flat, hand-riven (split rather than sawed) slats fitted into slots in the posts—indicative of a later stage of construction—and again packed with mud.

Once you have a basic idea of the building's construction, a documentation plan can be developed. Because the original section of the house may date to the

Fig. 39. Photo of the south and west elevations of the Brink-Wagner house, Oldenburg, Franklin County, Indiana. Photo by Thomas Carter.

first period of German occupation, its presence within the larger house is noteworthy. It should come as no surprise that the earliest buildings in any area are rare. Often small and insubstantial, such buildings are regularly demolished to make way for larger and more permanent ones. The old, however, is often embedded in the new, and a good place to look for evidence of early building types and construction technologies is within remodeled structures such as the Brink-Wagner house.

The remodeling is also important for it says a good deal about life in this immigrant community. The Wagners wanted a larger house, certainly, but it could not be just any house. When completed, the remodeling yielded a dwelling that was stylistically consistent with Anglo-American building practices in the region, a strategy for assimilation on the part of German immigrants whose newly constructed houses also matched Anglo-American designs.

Your decision, then, is to record the whole house with floor plans, a drawing of the principal elevation, construction elevations showing both original and newer timber-framing techniques, and sketches of the infill methods used on both sections. Record will also be made of the layout of the house lot on a site plan in order to show the kinds of outbuildings and other landscape features accompanying a small town house in the area.

The site plan usually comes first. After taping a sheet of 18" x 24" graph paper to your drawing board, create a title block in the lower right-hand corner of the sheet naming the drawing and giving the location of the building, the date of the fieldwork, and the names of the fieldworkers. Remember to label all your drawings since it is extremely easy to forget which building is which when you are drawing them up later. Next make a sketch of the house lot, showing the house on the corner and the workshop, woodshed, privy, well, large trees, orchard, and gardens (fig. 40). Because the house is associated with the store next door, the site plan will also show this building. Draw the site plan—and all other plans, elevations, and sections—as large as possible, filling up the entire sheet. Bigger drawings make for easier reading when you have many dimensions to record. At this point try to be as accurate as possible in positioning the buildings in relationship to each other so that when you begin to measure, your drawing is generally to scale with the actual distances being recorded. Pacing off the space between the buildings and other features on the lot yields rough dimensions that give some overall proportion to the field sketch.

With the site plan sketched out, now begin positioning the various features and adding measurements. If you have access to a surveyor's transit, this work is relatively quick and easy. For our purposes here, however, we will assume that you have only the basics: a hand-held compass and a measuring tape, which are enough to do the job. Begin recording the site by first establishing a datum—a fixed point on the lot from which all your angles and measurements will be made. If you can, find a datum from which you get an unobstructed view of all the features on the site and be sure that the datum you choose is durable enough so that later researchers can check your work. A natural feature, for example a large rock, or an important human product, such as a corner fence post, will do nicely. For the Brink-Wagner house, two datum points are required. The first, found at the corner of the lot, locates the house, store, and well. From a second datum, the well, the other features on the site can be positioned.

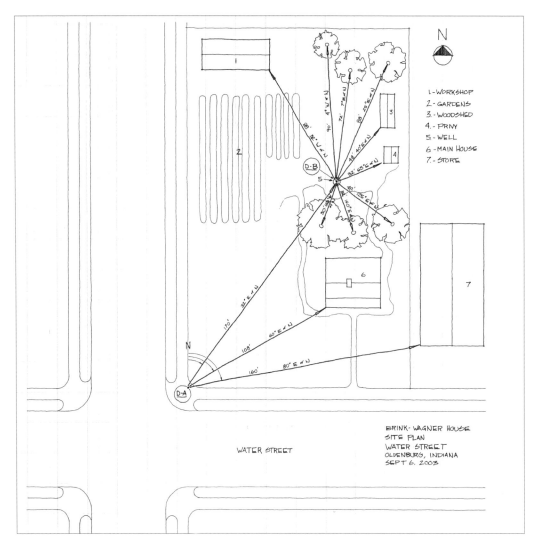

Fig. 40. Field sketch of the Brink-Wagner house site plan. Drawing by Yoshikazu Kono and James Gosney. Used by permission of the Western Regional Architecture Program, University of Utah.

To place elements on the site plan, stand at the datum and point the compass so that it reads due north. Then turn the dial so the directional indicator/arrow moves either to the left (west of north) or to the right (east of north) and so that it lines up with the nearest corner of the feature you want to position, noting the number of degrees off of north. In this way you can plot the various features in a circular motion—35 degrees west of north or 125 degrees west of north; or if you are going in the opposite direction, 80 degrees east of north or 260 degrees east of north. Whichever way you choose is fine, for the idea is to move in a circular manner so that when you lay the site out on a drawing board or computer you will be able to use a protractor, drawing compass, or CAD program to chart the various angles. Once the various angles are determined, then measure the distance along the compass readings, recording the length of the directional line leading from the datum to the feature being located. Next, measure the overall dimensions of each feature so that you will know how big they are, and then sight the compass along their sides to check their alignment on the lot. For the Brink-Wagner house, the work is fairly simple, but for a large site such as one of the German farms outside Oldenburg, Indiana, you will have more work to do.

After the site plan, floor plans come next. It is better to record the floor plans before you record the elevations and sections because the plan gives you most of the horizontal measurements you will need on the vertical drawings. Again, tape a large piece of graph paper to your board, label it, and start sketching out the layout of the building (fig. 41). In the days when floor plans were mostly used to establish typologies, the lower or ground floor plan was sufficient. Now that the emphasis in vernacular architecture research has shifted toward the use of space rather than pure

Fig. 41. Field sketch of the Brink-Wagner house ground plan. Drawing by Collin Tomb, Yoshikazu Kono, and James Gosney. Used by permission of the Western Regional Architecture Program, University of Utah.

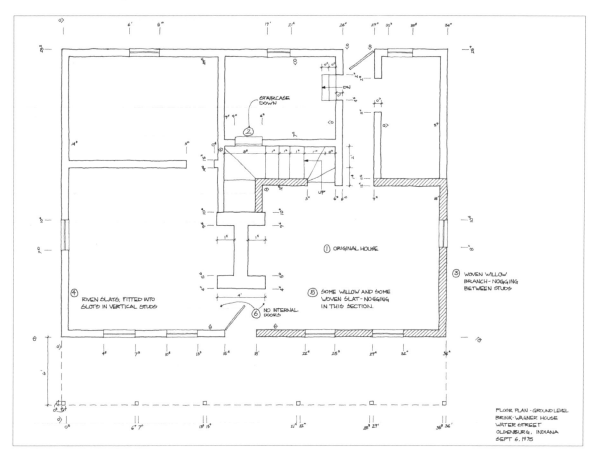

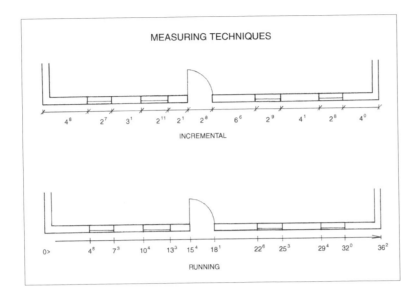

Fig. 42. Diagram showing running and incremental measuring systems. Schematic drawing by Yoshikazu Kono. Used by permission of the Western Regional Architecture Program, University of Utah.

taxonomy, the *entire* space should be recorded, and this means the main floor, the upper stories, the garret, and the basement if possible. Make your plan sketch as large as possible. For smaller buildings such as the Brink-Wagner house, one sheet for each floor is sufficient. For larger and more complex buildings, a sheet per room often works well. Sometimes, in situations when you have a great many measurements or fine details to draw, you will use up a lot of paper, but you will be glad you did when you start filling the sheets up with dimensions. Also, it is important to notice and record chronological sequences in the development of the building. A general rule is that materials are shown only in elevation and that on the plans such conventions as solid lines, cross-hatching, and stippling are used to indicate first, second, and third construction periods.

Do not be in a hurry to start measuring. Take time on all your field sketches to proportion things so that your drawing closely approximates the actual building. It is a good idea to do a preliminary overall measurement of both the width and depth of the plan, or of the height if you are doing an elevation. Then, knowing the basic size and height, you will be able to proportion the doors, windows, rooms, and so forth so that your sketch is a fairly accurate representation of the building. Then start measuring (fig. 42). *Running* measurements—which run continuously from start to finish—are the best to use because they are easy to lay out on a scale when you start drawing up your field notes. They leave less room for error since you are not repositioning the tape all the time, and they give an overall measurement at the end as a check on your work. The other way to measure is called *incremental,* by which you treat the distance between openings or other aspects of the buildings as discrete elements, each with its own measurement. Incremental measuring is recommended when the number of protrusions and other kinds of interruptions makes getting a complete run impossible (or very difficult), and this method is often used for interior spaces and on construction details and sections.

Returning to the Brink-Wagner house, start measuring at the lower left-hand (southwest) corner. The first recorded measurement will be a zero with an arrow (0>) pointing in the direction that the dimensions are being recorded. Then, using the running measurement technique, move to the right (east) noting down distances to the porch posts, the windows, and the door, and the overall length of the house in feet and inches. Do the same for the other walls, starting over each time with a 0> as indicated on the example (see fig. 41). On most plans, measure to the main openings and do not worry about the frames, casings, and moldings. If you want to include these details, take another sheet and draw up a representative window, door, or other desired building feature at a larger scale so that you can include it on your final drawing. Most architectural drawings will be produced at a ¼-inch scale, so the fine points are bound to get lost. We recommend measuring to the nearest ½ inch, however, mostly as an aid to quickly reading the tape. Always indicate inches as a superscript above the main foot number—3^6, 13^4, 29^7, and so forth; the symbols for feet (') and inches (") start looking like 1s and 11s and generally tend to add confusion to the drawing. Also, record numbers less than a foot—to be consistent—as "zero feet and seven inches" or as 0^7.

On the interior your work will be much the same. Take running measurements along the interior walls as noted on the example, recording the location of interior openings, partitions, and other features. Dimensions for openings on the outer walls are not needed since they have already been recorded from the outside. However, it is a good idea to take the dimensions for both the overall depth and the width of all rooms; these numbers will come in handy in checking your outside figures. Some incremental measuring will be needed around such things as the staircase and the fireplace, and to locate openings along those walls that did not require full recording. Be sure to measure the width of the outer and inner walls, measuring the width of the wall minus the door moldings. Write notes whenever they are needed, keying your observations to the sketch with circled numbers.

Fig. 43. Field sketch of the principal south elevation of the Brink-Wagner house without the porch. Drawing by Collin Tomb, Yoshikazu Kono, and James Gosney. Used by permission of the Western Regional Architecture Program, University of Utah.

Fig. 44. Setting the horizontal datum. Drawing by Yoshikazu Kono. Used by permission of the Western Regional Architecture Program, University of Utah.

Fig. 45. Setting the vertical datum. Drawing by Yoshikazu Kono. Used by permission of the Western Regional Architecture Program, University of Utah.

In recording elevations, the work turns vertical. Label a large field sheet and then sketch out the elevation as well as you can, again using some overall dimensions to help proportion your drawing (fig. 43). For the Brink-Wagner house, we have decided to draw only the principal elevation, although the basic technique would apply to the other elevations as well. Additionally, since the basic configuration of the facade openings needs to be illustrated, the shed-roofed porch that hides the lower elevation will not be sketched. Before starting to measure, you must first lay off horizontal and vertical datum lines, which are mandatory for elevation drawings because you cannot know that the house is on the straight and level. Set the horizontal datum with either a hand level or a transit at about the height of the foundation and then take all your measurements either above or below the line (fig. 44). A plumb bob can be used to set the vertical datum anywhere along the elevation (fig. 45). Then get a measurement from this line to the end of the nearest wall to establish a fixed reference for the elevation alignment.

Vertical running measurements may be taken using a tape and ladder or a measuring pole. Measuring poles, which are available from engineering supply stores in adjustable sizes, are considerably safer because they allow you to stay on the ground. Starting with another 0>, record distances to the principal vertical elements. Doors, windows, porches, and the like are important, but the distance to the top of the ridge and the height of the eaves are crucial dimensions because these two measurements give you the pitch of the roof. To keep things clear, it is often a good idea to do one set of measurements along the end of the building—to the ridge. Then add additional runs for the windows and doors. Recall that you already have most of the ground-level horizontal dimensions on the plan. Upstairs windows—front, sides, and rear—will most often have to be measured from the inside, although on the Brink-Wagner house the shed-roof porch provides a nice platform for running a tape across the upper portion of the building.

Reading the Physical Fabric

A crucial part of the architectural documentation process is learning to "read the building fabric," which is a way of saying that you must pay close attention to the way in which a building is constructed, what it is made of, how it has been embellished, and what changes have taken place. Construction, materials, and finishes all have their own stories to tell about a building's history and meaning. One attribute of drawing is that it makes you stop and take the time to carefully inspect the physical attributes—the fabric—of an architectural example so that you do not miss its most vital elements. As your recording work proceeds, concentrate on "getting your arms around the building," as one vernacular architecture fieldworker puts it, paying close attention to its details. You will not be sorry that you did.[13]

In looking at construction methods, it is best to start with a good working knowledge of the various kinds of technologies that would have been available to builders in your study community in different time periods. There are good surveys of American building methods that you can consult, and the literature on local and regional technologies is considerable. References to literature on construction methods

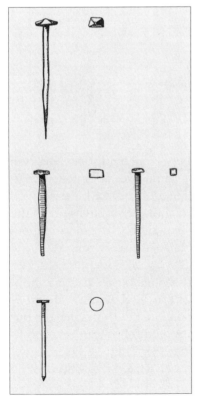

Fig. 46. Nail typology. Top: wrought nails generally used in the seventeenth, eighteenth, and early nineteenth centuries; middle: cut nails, from the 1790–1820 period; and lower: modern wire nails, 1835 to the present. From Gabrielle M. Lanier and Bernard L. Herman, *Everyday Architecture of the Mid-Atlantic: Looking at Buildings and Landscapes*, 94, fig. 3.31. Copyright © 1997. Reprinted by permission of The Johns Hopkins University Press.

can be found in the Vernacular Architecture Forum bibliography, which is published quarterly in the VAF newsletter, and in the journal of the Association of Preservation Technology (APT).[14]

The history of various industries—such as those producing nails, decorative millwork, and paints—is applicable to your work as well. For example, as nail fabrication shifted from hand to machine production during the late eighteenth century, nails changed appreciably in appearance. Handmade or "wrought" nails are irregularly shaped and have round or "rose" heads. Machine-made or "cut" nails have straight sides and t-shaped heads. If you find "cut" nails in your building and know when factory-produced nails were available in your study community, you can determine an approximate date for your structure. A similar shift occurred in the late nineteenth and twentieth centuries from cut to "wire" nails, providing another source for dating (fig. 46). Other industries that are good to know about are lumber (axes and adzes or hand-wielded pit saws, water-powered vertical-blade saws, and steam circular saws leave different and datable kinds of markings), heating (fireplaces were replaced by heating stoves, which in turn were supplanted), plumbing (tearing down the outhouse meant finding room in the building for a bathroom), building materials (check out when builders in your area would have had

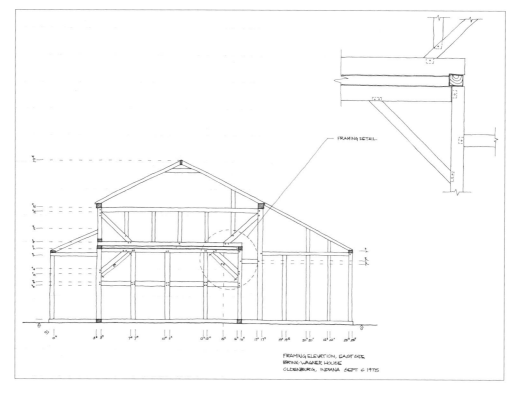

Fig. 47. Framing elevation field drawing, east end of the Brink-Wagner house, with detail sketch showing grafting of new second story onto the original house frame. Drawing by Collin Tomb, Yoshikazu Kono, and James Gosney. Used by permission of the Western Regional Architecture Program, University of Utah.

access to such things as concrete, aluminum siding, and linoleum), lighting, water, and so forth. The important thing to remember while you are recording a building is to develop a disciplined eye that looks for and registers various construction details for use during later stages of the analysis.[15]

Construction details are readily visible on the Brink-Wagner house because of its deteriorating condition. Nails and saw marks are not particularly useful for dating purposes here, however, since all sections have cut nails and blade marks left by the hand-hewing of the timbers. Both the older and newer sections of the house appear to have been heated, at least initially, by the fireplace opening into each of the front rooms. The wall framing techniques are another matter. As noted earlier, the initial inspection of the house indicated that the west and south sections were attached to what appears to have been the original structure—probably consisting of a single room, one story in height. When we look again at the construction methods of the two sections, it is possible to see differences that help substantiate the theory that the house went up in two distinct campaigns.

The framing on the east, when measured and drawn (fig. 47), shows itself to be the more complicated of the two systems. It has five studs mortised into a top end girt (or horizontal beam) and ground sill, and there are short girts placed halfway up the studs. On top of this frame is placed another one that appears quite separate. It rests on a set of second-story floor joists carried by the plate of the original section (see fig. 48). Angle braces secure the upper section to the lower one and are mortised into corner posts that carry the new roof. The method of infilling the spaces between the studs—often called "nogging"—is another indicator of the different dates for the east and west/upper sections of the house. Infilling on the east section consists of willow branches woven between upright slats. In the other walls the nogging is formed using hand-riven slats either woven between or slotted into the vertical studs. The apparent attachment of the west/upper frame to the smaller one on the east and the fact that the simpler (in that it takes less time to fabricate) woven-willow nogging is in the eastern part suggest that the house began as a single room—the east front section of the present building. This probably dates to the 1830s when German settlers moved into the area. At a later date, though probably not long after the initial construction (because all timbers are hand-hewn), the house was substantially enlarged, gaining a second story, six new rooms (counting two on the upper floor), a bracketed front porch, and finished exterior cladding.

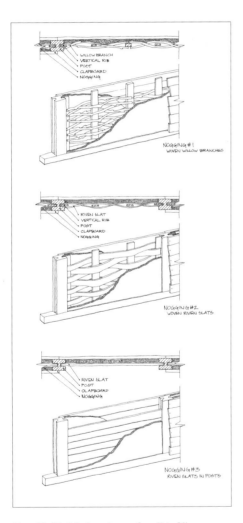

Fig. 48. Field sketches of wall infill or "nogging" systems found on the Brink-Wagner house. Drawing by Yoshikazu Kono and James Gosney. Used by permission of the Western Regional Architecture Program, University of Utah.

Material and finish techniques are also part of the diagnostic process, having the same kind of historical content as the methods of construction. Again, you should be aware of the literature pertaining to construction both in your study community and in the nation as a whole, for in the nineteenth century variously dimensioned lumber, brick, and metal building materials were widely distributed quickly. Knowing what kinds of materials were available and when, knowing what the cultural preferences of the people in the area were, and knowing how various elements were procured are all parts of the process of reading building fabric.[16]

Finishes—paint, moldings, flooring, mantels, and so forth—deserve the same kind of attention. You will find that the finish treatment of rooms will differ greatly by use—parlors and public spaces often received the finer finishes, while service areas are usually plain. You will also observe changes in preferred decorative styles. A good understanding of the possibilities for exterior and interior finishes in the time and place specific to the house is important as you inspect the building.[17]

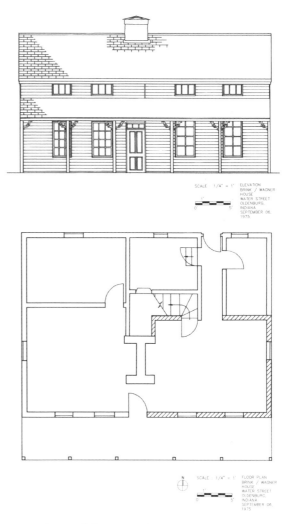

Fig. 49. Final drawings of the south elevation and principal ground plan of the Brink-Wagner house. Drawing by Yoshikazu Kono. Used by permission of the Western Regional Architecture Program, University of Utah.

All in a Day's Work

At least a full day would be required to complete the fieldwork on a building such as the Brink-Wagner house, and additional time—perhaps another day—will be needed to translate the field sketches into a finished architectural drawing (fig. 49). Vernacular architecture study requires a level of energy and commitment that only begins when you decide to talk to some owners about measuring their house. You have to keep reminding yourself that you are breaking new ground, studying buildings that indeed have never been studied before. And if you do not document them, no one else will. The Brink-Wagner house was demolished in the fall of 1980.

CHAPTER 3

A Framework
for Analysis

Your survey is done. You have measured and photographed a building or a set of buildings in your study area. Sometimes this may be enough; architectural documentation as an end in itself, after all, is a worthy pursuit. It is a good idea to get buildings recorded, especially if they are falling into disrepair or threatened with demolition. But drawing buildings, however valuable, is not the main concern of our work. As we said at the outset, vernacular architecture as a field of study is concerned with making informed inferences about what the built environment meant and continues to mean to the people who built and used it and to those who continue to build and use it. To move beyond description, the artifactual evidence must be ordered in such a way that interpretation can proceed. Common ordering systems—frameworks for analysis—in vernacular architecture studies are associated with time, space, form, function, and technology. Developing these analytical frames begins early in the data-gathering process and is the point at which the architectural and archival evidence join to reveal the patterns of behavior that are the goal of the research process.

Pattern is an important concept in vernacular architecture study because it results from repetition, and repetition—albeit with a healthy amount of variation and even innovation—is really what common buildings are all about. Consistency in the behavior of any group of people results, not from mindless imitation, but from the presence of a set of shared operating values. If something occurs once, it might be considered noteworthy, odd, or even amusing, depending on your perspective. But when whatever it is that you are observing occurs over and over again, then the repetitive behavior becomes a sign that this specific way of doing things was considered right and appropriate for a good many people at a specific time and over a defined space. Thus, through observing repetition we can decode the regular and patterned behavior that is culture.

For example, if we discover that a particular kind of two-room house was commonly found in eighteenth-century Virginia, it is quite possible, despite the individual eccentricities of the examples, to group them generally into a single typological category, calling them *hall-parlor* houses. Such a designation can be helpful in our analysis because the hall-parlor form can be traced back to English sources. It tells us not only that the idea for this type of dwelling made the transatlantic crossing but

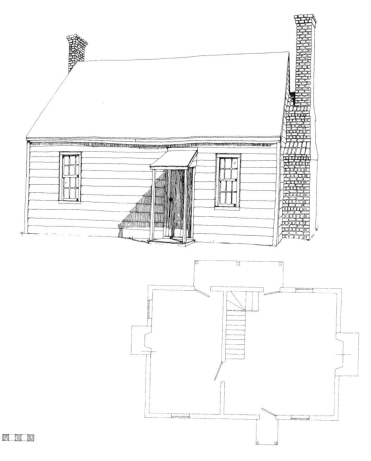

Fig. 50. The hall-parlor
house type, Port Royal,
Caroline County, Virginia.
Drawing by Henry Glassie
from his *Pattern in the
Material Folk Culture of
the Eastern United States*
(1968), 80. Reproduced by
permission of the Univer-
sity of Pennsylvania Press.
Copyright © 1968 by the
Trustees of the University
of Pennsylvania.

also that for the group of people who shared an English cultural background, two rooms—a hall for everyday living and a parlor where the parents slept and stored their best possessions—satisfied all their social and psychological needs (fig. 50).[1]

An obsession with pattern can, of course, place so much emphasis on the commonalities of culture that the true complexities of human existence are glossed over. Because there is so much variation in actual execution, the hall-parlor houses being investigated can also be viewed as discrete entities, each the product of very house-specific circumstances. From this point of view, the meaning of the house depends on which of its users you are talking about: the white male head of household, the eternally pregnant wife fixing dinner while the husband quaffs beer with his buddies, the white serving woman who is working off her indenture, or the African slave who lives in an even smaller house out back. Give the family some more money or make the wife a widow, have the roof of the house blow off, or free the slaves, and a whole new set of conditions arises that in turn demands a new set of interpretations. In short, the search for a single unified narrative works at one scale, but at another, where the rules of the game are constantly changing, the story fractures. This can become problematic as you find that for every generalization there can and will be an exception.[2]

Still, we need pattern. While there is little doubt that the past exists as a truly infinite number of powerful mininarratives—each of us, after all, plays our own little part in the larger story—the purpose of history is not well served by an interpretive scheme grounded in endless fragmentation. The lesson of recent historical scholarship is that indeed we must pay attention to the ways individual human experience is dramatically shaped by such things as class, gender, race, ethnicity, occupation, location—you name it and it will have a welcome place in the growing pantheon of historical frames of reference. Historical perspective is useful in knowing, for instance, how an economic elite preserves and perpetuates its power, what goes into the making and acceptance of gendered spaces, why racial segregation remains a fact of American life, and why a cyber-generation is obsessed with the search for authenticity. However, if we believe that history helps us understand better who we are, why we behave as we do, and where we might be heading in the future, then we still need to build models of interpretation that address how the central issues that do *not* divide us broadly shape the world we live in. One solution—a compromise—might be that when you build your mininarratives—the individual examples of architectural behavior that emerge from your fieldwork—aim toward collective statements of community structure and identity, toward interpretive narratives that tell about the ways people of all shapes and sizes, sexual orientations, skin colors, and nationalities try to survive in the world.

So while they may be open to endless qualification, the patterns are there and are revealed in the five main artifactual dimensions mentioned above: time, space, form, function, and technology. There is overlap among these, but each will be introduced and explained separately for the sake of clarity. In the following sections we also introduce techniques and procedures for elaborating the field data with supplementary historical information of all kinds. These two bodies of evidence—words and things—interweave to yield a composite portrait of the patterns of behavior we seek to uncover.[3]

Time

Chronology—dating a piece of architecture to a particular point in time or points in time (since most buildings, if they are not torn down, get used and reused many times)—is a fundamental part of vernacular architecture study. Knowing when a building was constructed or when it was remodeled establishes a time dimension for your study, and much of what you will do and say depends on these numbers. If you know that "at this time this happened," then you can proceed to ask such questions as "why this building—this behavior—at this time?" Chronology begins with dating, and while sometimes a builder might have been courteous enough to chisel the year of construction into stone or timber, finding the date will rarely be so easy. There is no single source that will attach dates to your buildings. Rather, there are many sources, and using them involves both commitment and hard work.

Dating buildings is like detective work. You follow leads anywhere you can get them in land records, tax rolls, probate inventories, court documents, private papers, architectural styles, construction technologies, and even building materials. All available evidence must be exploited, scraps of information pieced together, and facts checked against other facts; and no single source should be trusted, no matter how much you want to believe it. The imaginative use of a wide range of sources (with some luck thrown in) is what makes a successful architectural sleuth, and while there is no set procedure for dating and every locale will have its own quirky records, the following section outlines some things to consider as you move into the time dimension.

First of all, it is best to start the dating process as we did in chapter 2, with the investigation of the physical evidence. Know the basic architectural (exterior and interior) styles, building types, and technological systems well enough that your building or buildings can be placed in general chronological categories. Having a good idea of whether you are looking at a seventeenth-, eighteenth-, nineteenth-, or twentieth-century building limits the scope of your investigation considerably. For example, the presence of Georgian stylistic features typically places a building in the second half of the eighteenth century; Greek revival decorative finishes start appearing in American communities only after about 1830; the bungalow house type reached its greatest popularity during the first two decades of the twentieth century; balloon-framing techniques spread into general practice by the 1870s; and concrete as a principal material for building foundations and walls has been common only since 1900.[4]

In deriving dates by examining the building fabric, an archaeological term comes in handy: *terminus post quem* (the date after which).[5] The introduction into a geographical area of certain building types, styles, construction materials, or technologies can often be dated fairly precisely: that is, the idea for a new house type may arrive with a group of immigrants, a building style new to the area may be traceable to an architectural publication that appeared in a certain year, a local history might speak of the opening of a new quarry for producing limestone for buildings, or datable changes may occur in local technological systems. Be looking for changes in how materials are worked—we noted some of these above—such as the move from sash-type saw blades, which leave straight marks, to circular ones, which leave semicircular marks (fig. 51), and from hand-forged nails with irregular heads to cut nails, which are square, to wire nails, which are round. Detailed architectural description coupled with an idea of when particular forms and technologies became available in an area yield a "date after which" time element for the building you are studying.[6]

Information taken from the architectural analysis is then combined with data from, for example, land and tax records. From the beginning of European settlement, a public record was kept of land ownership. This is true for all parts of the country and for all time periods, from the early seventeenth century to the present. Located in various places—state archives, county courthouses, or city halls, depending on the locale—the land records do not themselves contain dates for buildings, but because buildings are necessarily tied to the land on which they sit, these documents, when used in conjunction with other kinds of information, are invaluable for dating buildings.[7]

Start your work in the land records with a description of the land on which your building stands. When you know where the building is located, you can then use the deed books, land transfer records, and other sources to trace the history of owner-

Fig. 51. The curved cut marks on this ceiling joist in central Utah were made by a water-powered circular saw blade. Photo by Thomas Carter.

ship for the property. Such a history is called a "chain of title," a chronologically arranged list of owners and their time of ownership. The chain of title opens up avenues for figuring out when a particular building on the property was constructed.

First, it may be that in researching the land records for your chain of title you will find specific references to the presence of buildings—usually called "improvements"—on the property at a certain date. This occurs most often in the earlier documents, those from the colonial era when clerks and other recorders took the time to describe the property being bought and sold. By the early nineteenth century the process of recording land transactions appears to have been reduced to its bare essentials—the listing of property boundaries and nothing else. Of course, even if you know that a building stood on the property at a certain time, you will not know its exact date of construction, nor will you necessarily know that the building you are interested in is the one described in the deed book. Here your architectural expertise will be your guide. If the records say that the house sat on a particular piece of ground in 1680, you must decide whether the house there now could be that old. If it could, then you are getting close to dating it. If not, your search must go on.

Another way the chain of title can be used for dating buildings is through the names of the owners. Again, the appearance and construction of the house will give you a rough idea of its date, and from this you can investigate the people who resided there during these years. They may show up in the local tax rolls being assessed for "improvements" to their property, which may include a house or other kind of building. A family diary or journal may be found that speaks of a house being constructed in a particular year. Local newspapers and histories may also contain passages relating to the construction of certain buildings, and these will most often be identified by their owners. Again, you will have to determine if the architecture of your house matches the date given it in the documents, but the likelihood is good that it will and that you have arrived, albeit in a circuitous fashion, at the date you are looking for.

A construction date may also be inferred from the chain of title by looking for significant changes in the valuation of the property. This technique is particularly useful after the nineteenth century, when records became less intimate but more quantifiable. Say, for instance, that a person buys a property in 1910 for three hundred dollars and sells it 1920 for three thousand dollars. In all likelihood, the small bungalow that now stands on the site was built for the family sometime between 1910 and 1920. You may also find important clues to building dates in the legal instruments attached to the transactions, particularly the mortgages, for if the person who bought the property above took out a sizable mortgage in 1913, we might conclude that the bungalow was built specifically in that year.

Dating is also possible through other sources. Town or county building departments or county clerks may keep records of construction and alterations through building permits, tax assessment records, and probate inventories. Maps, as we have seen, can also be an invaluable resource in dating buildings, telling you when a particular building shows up on the landscape. You can also look through diaries, journals, letters, and other kinds of unpublished personal documents for building dates, though as we have seen above, this kind of search is most productive when you have some specific names. Dendrochronology, a system for dating based on comparing wood core samples from historic buildings with a master tree ring chart, and the systematic analysis of historic paint layers are also gaining wider use as analytical techniques become more sophisticated.[8]

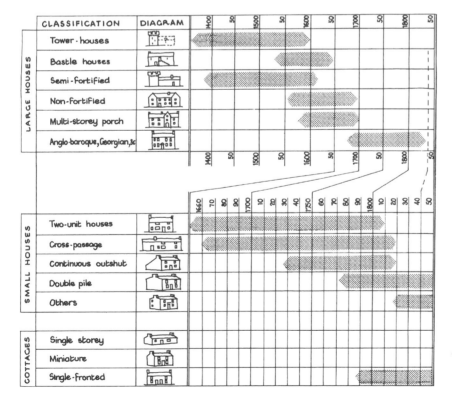

Fig. 52. Seriation study graphing typological change along a time line. From R. W. Brunskill, *Traditional Buildings of Cumbria: The County of the Lakes* (London: Cassell & Co., 2002), 189. Reprinted by permission.

Fig. 53. Architectural seriation in the landscape: trailer house and I-house, Franklin County, North Carolina. Photo by Thomas Carter.

Fig. 54. Architectural seriation in a single house: exploded axonometric drawing showing the sequence of construction campaigns in the Andrew N. Olsen house, Spring City, Utah. Drawing by Jeff Davis and Roberto Pinon. Used by permission of the Western Regional Architecture Program, University of Utah.

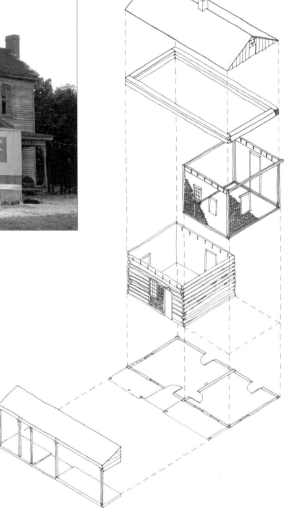

After carefully dating the collected architectural data, you are now ready to order it so that patterns of behavior are revealed. One strategy taken from archaeological practice, *seriation,* is applicable to your work. Seriation is a tactic for plotting a series of examples along a time line. The purpose of this graph is to show the changes in various types of buildings, styles, technologies, functions, etc., through time (fig. 52). Seriation works best when you have a larger number of dated individual properties or sites which, when arranged along a time line, illuminate the pattern of architectural change or the lack of it in your study community.[9]

Seriation is also visible in the "layering" of architectural styles or types within a given building or study community.[10] The original architecture in most areas—and in most buildings, too, that endure long enough to be used and reused—gets added onto over time by the continual appearance of newer buildings and building elements.

Building and rebuilding and further rebuilding (and remodeling) leave behind within a given community or individual building layers or "strata" of architectural activity, each differing in such things as style, materials, technology, or function (figs. 53 and 54). These layers can be identified and dated. Seriation, using a number of buildings or simply looking for time sequences within a single property or building, provides a mechanism for ordering your data sequentially so that you can begin to explain the causes behind each new architectural deposit.

Space

Individual buildings occupy space and may be mapped so that others will know where your examples are located. Another good reason for taking the time to do a survey is to place your data geographically so that you begin to see how your buildings are distributed spatially in your study community. Once constructed, buildings form a series of contextual relationships with other buildings that may be mapped in such a way that consistencies in behavior—patterns again—are made evident. It is in showing the distribution of your assembled data according to such things as time, class, race, gender, ethnicity, or construction technology (to name a few of these relationships) that the power of maps lies.[11]

Chronologically organized maps are an obvious by-product of the dating process outlined in the above discussion of seriation, and are produced by discovering the various periods of architectural development in the study community, whether it is geographically or thematically defined. Mapping the time dimension of your data may be used to illuminate such things as the location of the newer and the older sections of a town (the older section is perhaps found nearest the source of water or a transportation route, while the new parts are often on the suburban peripheries), architectural changes in a particular farmstead or town (several sequential maps can effectively be used to diagram these changes), and even the movement or diffusion of particular building practices through both time and space—buildings or technologies from a later date, when plotted on the map, show a steady progression across the land over time.

The cultural landscape, as we have seen, is also differentiated according to a range of socially determined categories. Wealth is one such distinction and is evident in such things as the distribution of houses in a community according to size: big, medium-sized, and little houses can be mapped in such a way that elite, middle-class, and working class neighborhoods become readily discernable. Such patterns vary according to time and place—mansions, for instance, may be found near the center of town, close to the sources of economic and civic power, or placed on adjacent hillsides so that they can look down over people of lesser status. Work in the historical records can also help to verify the spatial relationships of wealth, for you can determine the value of individual households by locating the owners—which you identified in the title search—in county, city, or federal tax rolls, which give a family's net worth.[12]

The mapping of race and ethnicity may be accomplished by marking the locations of certain racially and ethnically affiliated building types, such as dwellings for slaves on southern plantations, the French-American Creole house along the Mississippi River, the black-kitchen houses of Slovenians on the Great Plains, or the Polish-American social clubs found in New England cities. The clustering of examples points out where concentrations of these racial or immigrant populations were or still are. Construction technologies like log corner-notching, timber framing, and masonry also often have definite ties to ethnic identity and provide possible mapping opportunities. The larger landscape is often organized by race and ethnicity through self- or legislated segregation. The occurrence of such areas, marked by the prevalence of certain architectural elements, is verified by additional demographic data found in the federal census schedules (which indicate race and place of birth for all the inhabitants of a particular household). These enclaves can be effectively indicated through the mapping process.[13]

Female space is often less obvious in the landscape, a fact of the essentially patriarchal structure of our society. Houses are usually identified with the male head of household, and are often in fact named in the historical literature for the man in the family—the John or James or Frank Doe House—as if he were the only person who lived there. The workplace too, until recently, has been a male-controlled domain, with access to it and the power such access bestows largely denied to women. The mapping of gender usage of space might center on the way that men during the work day are the predominant users of urban space and women of the suburbs,[14] how traditional

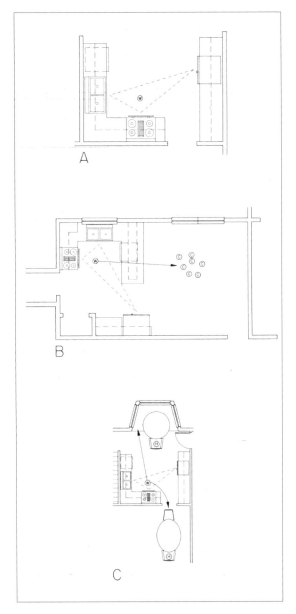

Fig. 55. These three kitchen plans are from 1970s-era ranch houses found in Layton, Utah. Interviews with the occupants, coupled with observations of daily use, reveal how these spaces are organized along gender lines: A. this "convenience triangle" contains sink, stove, and refrigerator, with space in the middle for the wife; B. a low countertop visually opens the family room to the eye of the wife/mother so that she can watch the children while preparing meals; C. the wife's seat in the breakfast nook and her chair at the dining table facilitate access to the work areas and make waiting on the husband easier. Fieldwork and drawings by Chamonix Larsen Wilson with help from James Gosney. Used by permission of the Western Regional Architecture Program, University of Utah.

household spaces are organized to reinforce responsibilities that are divided along gendered lines,[15] or how the placement of appliances, play areas, and furniture reinforces traditional subservient roles for women in the modern ranch house (fig. 55).[16]

Building types—industrial, commercial, educational, religious, recreational, or residential—when indicated on a map are a good source of information concerning the various zones of human activity in that area. Again, the census schedules[17] are helpful in showing the demographic contours of your study area because they also include in their listings occupations for all adult members of the household; county gazetteers and city directories also list occupation. Where do people work? Where do they shop? Where do they play? Where do they live? And do families group themselves by specific occupation—miner, machinist, laborer—within the residential zones? These are all relevant research questions that can be addressed and even answered by mapping your assembled data.

Form

The study of common buildings revolves around the analysis of physical form, whether in the shape of an individual building, a community of buildings, or an entire cultural landscape. The built environment is certainly like a text, although one that, like any book in another language, takes some time and special training to read. In working through the intricacies of the architectural language, two concepts—*style* and *type*—are particularly instructive. Both have long been associated with architectural history in all its various guises, and a familiarity with both is essential for work in vernacular architecture.

Style

Following the lead of architectural historian Dell Upton, who confronts the definitional puzzle of architectural style directly in several essays, it is possible to gather the current uses of the term *style* into two main areas.[18] On one hand, style is viewed as a unifying force in architecture—visible as a constancy of form—that emanates from the deep cultural subconscious. Style in this definition works as an ordering system, a kind of aesthetic philosophy, that people use to "address deep, often unarticulated, cultural principles for organizing and classifying experience."[19] In the realm of values, beliefs, and ideals, we find ourselves looking for a building's essential qualities, irrespective of decorative frills and other such superficialities. And if we look at style in this way, Upton suggests, there may be just two styles or aesthetic philosophies to worry about: the classical, which is "regular, ordered, modular, symmetrical, balanced"; and the picturesque, which is "less obviously ordered, asymmetrical, less obviously unified, often accretive."[20] The rational is played off against the emotive (fig. 56).

The other popular definition of *style* that Upton identifies is based not on the artifact's ability to unify but rather on its capacity to divide. Architectural styles under this heading are most often associated with changing aesthetic impulses and march through

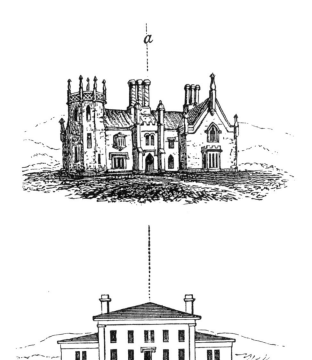

Fig. 56. Diagram showing the two principal aesthetic philosophies: the picturesque and the neoclassical. From Andrew Jackson Downing, *[Victorian] Cottage Residences* (1873; reprint, New York: Dover, 1981), 19.

time as the Georgian style, the Federal, the Greek revival, the Gothic revival, the Italianate, the Queen Anne, and so forth up to the present (fig. 57).[21] *Style,* when it is interpreted this way, refers to a combination of design features that divide architectural behavior into discrete categories that signify various tastes and social divisions within a given community. Style thus becomes a vehicle for distinguishing one set of things from another—or better, differentiating between particular behaviors—and rather than the two integrating stylistic philosophies, the classical and the picturesque, found in the first definition of *style,* we have multiple styles in the second definition.

For the purposes of this guide, we prefer a definition of *style* that makes it as flexible as possible—that is, one that combines the best of both definitions. Style is not particularly one thing or another, but rather a remarkably fluid concept that implies both a degree of formal constancy, which has a unifying effect within a culture, and formal deviation, which serves to distinguish various subcultures within the whole, depending on the situation. Both can be present in the same object. Art historian Jules Prown simply says that "the way in which something is done, produced, or expressed is its *style,*" and this may not be a bad way of looking at it either, for viewing style as an action, even as a type of artistic performance, works well in vernacular architectural studies. It directs our attention away from the nuances of classification to the way people use buildings and landscapes to represent themselves in the world (fig. 58).[22]

In a consumer society—one based on the belief that "you are what you have"—buildings say much about their builders and users. Personal and community identity alike are socially constructed and reconstructed through the acquisition and display of objects. The ways in which these objects are "done, produced, or expressed"—in short, their *styles*—play a crucial role in the representational process. We read buildings and landscapes most easily through their stylistic qualities, and these are observable on several levels, from the deepest cognitive formulations of the classical and picturesque to the most apparent and seemingly superficial expressions of ornamentation.[23]

Do not be in a hurry to judge which is more important, for both functions of style—the integrating and the differentiating—are useful when it comes to deciphering the architectural text. For example, two houses from the Boston area, one from the middle years of the eighteenth century and the other from the very end of that century, share the balanced symmetry of classical style that helped their owners adhere to the accepted standards for gentility and refinement prevailing through this era. Yet, the earlier house (fig. 59), on the surface, is embellished and ornate, while the other, later one (fig. 60) is plainly austere, a difference that speaks of the move not only from the Georgian architectural style to the Federal style, but also from an older aristocratic and definably English style to a newer and more businesslike bourgeois stylistic sensibility that emerged within the city's elite. In both Boston area houses, style was an important consideration throughout the designing process, expressing in both cases the values of the individual owners and how such values changed in the city over time.[24]

Treated in this way, style also helps break down the qualitative distinctions between academic architecture and vernacular architecture. As we have pointed out, the gap between the two is largely a factor of economics—the amount of money the builder has

Fig. 57. Changing architectural taste in Pennsylvania: on the right is a geometrically contained house, c. 1870, in the classical spirit; the house on the left, dating to the 1890s, is stylistically picturesque with Victorian eclectic decorative features. Photo by Thomas Carter.

Fig. 58. Style as identity: wall mural at the corner of Lake and Pico in the Hispanic Pico-Union section of Los Angeles. Photo by William Carter.

to spend on the project. That being said, however, it should be pointed out that such "high" and "low" distinctions within a particular stylistic tradition are ideal mechanisms for discovering class differences within your study community. Rather than worrying about whether a particular building is a good or an inferior example of a style, we should be thinking of how people used their available financial resources to try to fit in or to create boundaries between themselves and others (see chapter 1, figs. 16 and 17).

Type

The other concept that is used to analyze form is *type* and its correlate *typology,* a system of types. A *type* can be defined as a group of objects having certain traits or features in common. Types and typologies are usually used in architectural studies to gather sets of similar buildings into manageable units for the purposes of study, and

Fig. 59. Georgian classicism is reflected in the sculptural qualities of the John Vassal house, 1759, Cambridge, Massachusetts. Photo by Thomas Carter.

Fig. 60. Federal-era sensibilities reinterpret the classical in a flat, more austere style in the first Harrison Gray Otis House, 1795–96, Boston, Massachusetts. Photo by Thomas Carter.

Fig. 61. Center Mill, c. 1826, Slatersville, Rhode Island. Photo by Thomas Carter.

it is usually up to the researcher—somewhat arbitrarily—to determine what the distinguishing elements will be. The types that you choose as your analytic tools are, however, inherently tied to culture. For example, typologies common in American architectural research include use categories such as churches and form categories such as hall-parlor houses or skyscrapers. If we were in another culture our types might be "summer buildings" or "buildings that animals may not enter."[25]

Probably the most common architectural typologies are those associated with building uses, which although they have a formal component, remain primarily fixed on function. Familiar *types* of buildings grouped by function are houses, barns, churches, city halls, factories, sports stadiums, and so forth (fig. 61). Size, shape, and materials will vary, and there are often great discrepancies within such typologies, but types are important as starting points in a great deal of research, particular in looking at design precedents.

A useful analytic tool in vernacular architecture studies is the formal type. Formal types may be considered subcategories—subtypes—of the larger functional types. There are, that is, many "house" types, "church" types, and "barn" types, depending on the formal characteristics of a building. Generally, formal typologies are based on the most unchanging of a building's features, which would in many cases be the building's overall shape (rectilinear, circular, and so forth), its orientation or presentation (broad or narrow side to the street), and its plan (one room, two rooms, two rooms with a rear kitchen, and the like). These features we call *primary characteristics* in order to distinguish them from *secondary characteristics,* which include highly variable elements such as construction techniques and materials, decorative elements such as trim and color, and even use, which can change over time and can change without affecting the integrity of the type itself (fig. 62).[26]

Typologies are useful in several ways as you prepare your data for analysis. They may be ordered spatially by mapping, so that patterns of diffusion or movement of ideas are illustrated. Placed within the time dimension, they yield chronological sequences—seriations—that allow us to see how values and behaviors change or do not change through time. Chronologically ordered typologies are used by architectural historians and architects in understanding precedents for new designs, and certainly in vernacular architecture they work this way as well, for once defined, functional and formal types often are found to have long histories of their own. For example, the American schoolhouse, a functional type, has gone through a myriad of formal transformations. One-room schools, where all the students were grouped together, have evolved into multiroom schools that separate students by age, skill, or subject to be studied. Noting changes in a type leads to asking questions about why such changes have occurred.

Function

Function is one of the most complex aspects of a building's identity. Because vernacular buildings are often plain and unpretentious in comparison with their academic cousins, it

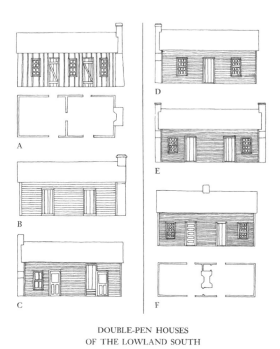

DOUBLE-PEN HOUSES
OF THE LOWLAND SOUTH

Fig. 62. Type and variation in the double-pen houses of the Lowland South. Schematic drawing by Henry Glassie from his *Pattern in the Material Folk Culture of the Eastern United States,* 103. Reproduced by permission of the University of Pennsylvania Press. Copyright © 1968 by the Trustees of the University of Pennsylvania.

has been easy to view them as products of practical utility: *form,* as the saying goes, follows *function,* with function in this sense being defined narrowly as something growing from the building's primary use as shelter. A functional house is one that keeps out the rain, warms its inhabitants, and provides enough room for eating and sleeping. Certainly, common buildings function in these ways—all architecture does. But it is not all they do, as Henry Glassie and others have pointed out. "If we choose to begin with the artifact," Glassie writes, "then our first goal should be the attempt to face the thing, not as a usable entity or mere object, but as a sign, as the result of an intention."[27] Human intentions in architecture are multifaceted, to say the least, and the resulting architecture has many levels of function (fig. 63).

What we ask our buildings to do for us is not insignificant. In an older book that warrants continued attention, Christian Norberg-Schulz suggests that architecture functions in four dimensions: first, the *physical control* of the natural environment, including the regulation of "climate, light, sound, and smell"; second, the *functional frame* for the human actions that "take place within a building's walls," actions that determine the size, form, and meaning of those spaces; third, the *social milieu* where the building "transcends" the functional frame to materially express such things as economic status, inclusion in or exclusion from a group, a particular role in society, or even the "social system as a whole"; and fourth, the task of *cultural symbolization,* in which architecture is used to embody and make manifest the deeper values and beliefs that provide both structure and meaning to everyday life.[28]

How can you determine the specific function of the building you are studying in each of these various dimensions? Some evidence, particularly in the social and cultural areas, comes from the careful analysis of the architectural fabric, through field documentation. But social and cultural functions may also be conveyed by visual representations of interior spaces. For nineteenth-, twentieth-, and twenty-first-century buildings, handy sources include historic photos (found in family albums or archive collections), trade catalogs and advice manuals, and the prescriptive reform literature.[29]

Another way of discovering the functions of a building is by looking in the biographical sources—learning about the people who lived in the buildings you are studying. Personal documents, such as letters from or to the occupants, often remark on aspects of use. Owners and builders also use sketches to communicate with each other about proposed new buildings or additions to existing ones, and these can contain useful information about the intended function of the architecture. You should also check personal diaries for records of experiences by those living in a specific dwelling. Travelers, too, often describe in their journals the buildings they see or stay in, providing in the process vignettes of the kinds of activities that take place in certain spaces.

Fig. 63. A multifunctional late nineteenth-century store in South Pass City, a mining town in west central Wyoming. The building's functions include keeping out the weather and providing the owner with a place to sell merchandise. The false-front facade—a frame attachment is placed over the log walls of the building—is used both to announce that this is a commercial building, as opposed to a house, and to lend an air of civilized respectability to this frontier commercial establishment. Photo by Thomas Carter.

The names people give to their spaces also help us determine use. Room names are tied to specific functions, and these can be found in personal documents such as those described above. They can also be found in public records, for instance probate inventories made on the death of a house owner. These inventories, which list the contents of a house by room, tell us not only what each room contained but also what the names of the rooms were in that house. The kinds of furnishings found in a room and the name given to the space suggest the way that room was used. The locations of other kinds of goods help us to interpret the uses that the rooms supported and help us approach an understanding of how the house worked for its occupants.[30]

Clues about intention are also found in the interior architecture. The presence of finely executed moldings, decorative framing members, and fancy painting may indicate that a room was planned as a public space—a place for entertaining and impressing visitors. Similarly, workrooms and accommodations for boarders, servants, and slaves may be separated from the center of activity and small in size and mean in finish when compared to the spaces inhabited by family members. These adjustments in room finishes alert us to class hierarchies defined and reinforced by the architecture.[31]

Technology

As students of buildings, vernacular architecture researchers have from the beginning been fascinated with construction technologies. By technology, we mean the various systems available for putting together a building so that it will be able to carry out the functions required by its builders, owners, and users. All kinds of materials and construction methods are studied, ranging from the hand-crafted and traditional to the modern and mass-produced (figs. 64 and 65).

As in other areas of research, technological systems must first be described, dated, and mapped in such a way that patterns of use, chronology, and distribution may be observed. A good deal of published material exists in this area, so you should become acquainted with the literature concerning the technologies available in the architectural community you are investigating. These sources will not only help you better understand how buildings are constructed, but they will also help establish a time frame for dating your examples.

While technology often seems relegated to the first function in our list—the physical control of nature—it can play a role in the social and cultural arenas as well. For example, there has always been a social hierarchy of building materials. In the eighteenth century brick stood at the top, while the more natural materials such as log and stone were at the bottom (see fig. 4 in the introduction). During the middle years of the twentieth century, aluminum siding as an exterior wall covering was often valued as a durable, low-maintenance product of modernity. By the 1990s, however, its stock had fallen and more natural materials such as wooden shingles, rusticated stone, and even log were held in greater esteem. Buildings are extremely complex texts in which the mediums may carry powerful messages.

Fig. 64. Early nineteenth-century V-notch log construction at the Fruit Hill Plantation, Kentucky. Photo by Thomas Carter.

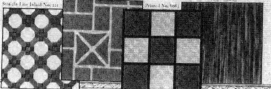

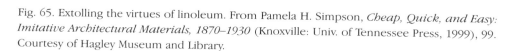

Fig. 65. Extolling the virtues of linoleum. From Pamela H. Simpson, *Cheap, Quick, and Easy: Imitative Architectural Materials, 1870–1930* (Knoxville: Univ. of Tennessee Press, 1999), 99. Courtesy of Hagley Museum and Library.

CHAPTER 4

Vernacular Architecture Studies: Interpreting the Data

Like Sally in the *Peanuts* cartoon (fig. 66), those of us who are interested in historical architecture have to recognize that we were not there when it happened, when the buildings were built and initially used. Unless the builders or residents are still alive, we cannot know what the people who lived in and used them were thinking, or why they did things the way they did. We do have the buildings, however, as an unmediated record of their actions. History is not a science but rather an artful attempt to use evidence from the past not only to tell us what happened but, in the end, also why it happened so that we can learn from what we have done to gain perspective on present problems.

So history depends on interpretation. We have evidence of past actions and events, and it is up to us to explain them—to make them understandable. The best that we can do is to come up with a rigorous method for assembling our data, so as to avoid random and impressionistic commentary. The research method outlined in the preceding pages is designed with that goal in mind, to provide a practicable and systematic approach to studying historic buildings. In the final analysis, the interpretation is up to us. We have to decide what this stuff means, for there is no inherent truth. And as we have seen, old buildings, like their dead occupants, cannot speak for themselves. We speak for them, knowing of our responsibility.

Fig. 66. *Peanuts* cartoon. Used by permission of United Media.

What this means, of course, is that history is always also about us as interpreters, for we bring our own particular views or ways of seeing the world to the table. Vernacular architecture emerged as a scholarly endeavor during the turbulent 1960s and 1970s, a time of social activism and reform. When the field was developing, older ideas about architecture as art were being questioned, and a new attitude was coalescing around a concern for common people and what their buildings may say about them. The inquiries of present and future generations of interpreters will be driven by other philosophical or moral commitments. And you will select theories or points of view that will best serve your own particular position when you construct your interpretations of the built environment.

No matter how hard you try, interpretation cannot occur without theory—some sort of intellectual frame that orients the data toward explanation. Our work starts with observation and description, looking carefully at the buildings and documenting their properties. However, a careful description does not get us far toward understanding human behavior. To move beyond description, we need theories to assist the interpretive process. Your gathered data, described and sorted, can be imagined as a building with many doors that can be entered from different directions. The kind of story elicited from observations of the building changes according to which door we want to enter—that is, our point of view and the types of issues we want to explore. Issues may be approached from a variety of historical, philosophical, or political viewpoints and supplemented with information from numerous other disciplines. Theories stand between the object and the interpretation. We observe our data through a theory and begin to formulate our story of what happened.

The following section will describe how some contemporary scholars have opened different doors, applied different lines of questioning to the evidence gleaned from buildings, and come up with fresh interpretations. The approaches will start with the concept of building type, then consider the materials and craft of construction and interior finish, move on to the scale of plan and room relationships, expand to exterior style, and then explore buildings in their immediate and larger landscapes. Along the way we will mention interpretations that make claims about larger-scale, more abstract cultural and social relationships. To support diverse points of view in analyzing vernacular architecture, we will identify publications by various scholars who have used these interpretive strategies successfully. The scholarship summarized here offers avenues for further reading. As architectural examples unfold under these diverse interpretations, you will see that vernacular architecture has enormous potential for telling us about the peoples, values, and cultures of the American landscape.

Building Types and Typologies

We encountered the concept of a "building type" earlier—a way to identify a building by naming its function in combination with the repertoire of forms that a specific culture uses for that function. Fruitful studies of vernacular architecture have been made by selecting a particular building type for investigation. Comparing several examples of a building type yields an understanding of potential variables within the type, while comparisons with other types help to illuminate the meanings that accrue to the example, making it distinctive.

Using the concept of *building type* to isolate a particular New England house form, Kingston Heath studied the "triple-decker," a house type common in Massachusetts in the early twentieth century. This form emerged to satisfy demands for blue-collar workers' housing in an industrializing era. Heath's recent book *The Patina of Place* examines the triple-decker as a physical form, analyzes its spatial elements, and alerts us to the way this house type was used to construct whole neighborhoods.[1] Heath's principal interest is in examining the ways that triple-deckers were used and changed by their inhabitants. Working-class families capitalized on the three independent, yet linked units in a triple-decker house to keep extended families connected to each other. Children were in and out of numerous household units in their own and neighboring triple-deckers during the day as they visited aunts, were fed by grandmothers, or dropped in on their playmates (fig. 67). Changes in family fortunes could be accommodated by families taking in a widowed parent or an unemployed uncle, making use of the flexibility inherent in the triple-decker's room adjacencies, circulation patterns, and roomy porches. Heath's deep examination of a building type allows him to uncover all the variety contained within a seemingly repetitive physical form. By choosing to look at his building type through the lens of family relations and their changes over time, he illuminates aspects of building performance—the way the building worked for its inhabitants—that previous historians have missed.

Starting with the concept of the house as a building type, Gabrielle Lanier and Bernard Herman identify multiple subtypes, variations on house forms,

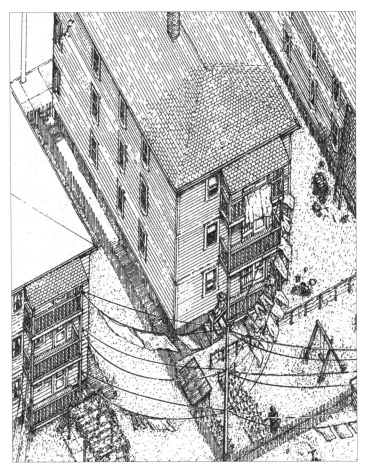

Fig. 67. Axonometric view of a Rhode Island three-decker house. Three households rented floors in this dwelling type, which enabled families to have independence while sustaining connections with relatives and friends. From Kingston Wm. Heath, *The Patina of Place: The Cultural Weathering of a New England Industrial Landscape* (Knoxville: Univ. of Tennessee Press, 2001), 13. Reproduced by permission of the author.

in their book *Everyday Architecture of the Mid-Atlantic.*[2] They develop *typologies of form*—that is, a systematic description of the possible divisions of space in both house plans and site plans—prevalent in the eighteenth and nineteenth centuries. Their simplest typological division in the common architecture of Delaware and contiguous states is between the open plan and the closed plan—that is, between the house that is open to direct access from the outdoors into a heated room and the house that can only be entered in stages, first into an unheated vestibule or passage and then into a heated room. They then go on to identify the open-plan types—hall or one-room plans, two-room plans, three- and four-room plans—and then the closed-plan types. Establishing such typologies allows a scholar to group or categorize buildings and to take lessons from the aggregate. Open-plan types, following Henry Glassie's earlier interpretation, are open to penetration directly, and are therefore associated with communities in which people have close interpersonal relationships and freely enter each other's houses. Closed plans make the visitor penetrate the house in stages, and are associated with communities in which a social system based on rank establishes order for both strangers and inhabitants.[3] Making connections between typical spatial arrangements in common building subtypes and typical community relations allows us to see buildings as indicators of major social shifts.

Familiarity with the existing building types of a time period or region will make *new building types* easy to identify as they appear on the vernacular architecture horizon. The office building was a new building type of the late nineteenth century whose multiple repeating floor plans, elevations, and vertical circulation patterns were all new to American architecture. This type came as a response to the separation of white-collar bureaucratic work from blue-collar labor in the later nineteenth century. The cultural norms of that period shaped the ways that the office building's spaces would be used. The historian Angel Kwolek-Folland, in her book *Engendering Business: Men and Women in the Corporate Office 1870–1930,* explores the ways that white-collar work, new to the 1870s, relied on Victorian notions of the place of women as the "weaker sex." Translated into business practices, this meant that as the office labor force was divided into "managerial or 'brain' workers and clerical or 'manual' workers," women were assigned to the latter and understood to have lesser skills and therefore correspondingly lower pay. It followed that the space of newly conceived sky-scraper office buildings was also gendered, with large aggregate spaces allotted to female secretarial pools and individual offices given to male managers. Likewise men's and women's restrooms were spatially interpreted. In the 1916 Victor Talking Machine Building in Camden, New Jersey, the men's toilets were located on every floor and near the public reception area since men actively used all the spaces of the office building, while the women's toilets were only on every other floor and as far from the main reception area as possible, making women's presence in the workforce more invisible. This display of differential spaces for men and women permanently instilled in and reinforced to all users the differential values placed on men's and women's work in the new office building type.[4]

Scholars who have focused on the concept of building type have arrived at diverse and fruitful interpretations through this avenue. Isolating a specific triple-decker type and analyzing its changes over time in response to habitation gives us a new sense of the flexibility of a type formerly seen as rigidly repetitive. Looking for patterns of spatial divisions or subtypes within the free-standing house yields relationships to community norms. Inquiry into a new building type, the office building, reveals the way it mirrors extant gender relations in society even as it attempts to accommodate new kinds of work.

Building Materials and Craft

While the concept of building type tells us about the combined form and function of a building, it tells us nothing about what a building is made of or how it is constructed. Building materials, craft processes, and the production and location of ornament tell us more about the culture that made a building. These craft issues have provided a category of analysis for scholars interested in what buildings are made of, how they are fabricated, and what that means. In the United States there is a long tradition of building in wood, a material plentiful at the time of first settlement. Early houses were constructed using wood in the form of logs. A popular method was to build by stacking the logs so that they overlapped at their corners, making a solid wall. Another method was to stand the logs vertically on sills to make a wall. Log construction has remained popular for American houses from the seventeenth century into the twentieth century and can even be chosen today as a building material available in prefabricated house kits. Alternatively wood can be cut into variously dimensioned pieces and used to build a frame. The frame is open, covered on the exterior with some kind of cladding, and usually covered on the interior as well. Seventeenth- and early eighteenth-century frames were made of heavy timbers, widely spaced and mortised and pegged together; later eighteenth- and early nineteenth-century frames used smaller timber sections and simpler joints; while frames of the industrialized era such as balloon frames were made from light wood pieces cut in sawmills to regular sizes, closely spaced, and nailed together. These materials could be mass-produced by factories and millwork shops, and shipped to distribution points by rail.

Researchers have investigated vernacular architecture through its building materials and construction methods to reach several different interpretations. An essay by Fred Kniffen and Henry Glassie, "Building in Wood in the Eastern United States: A Time-Place Perspective," suggests that the different methods of building in wood and especially different techniques for log building are attached to different ethnic groups.[5] Because the technique used for notching the corners of logs is quite specific to each ethnic tradition, the building material is impressed with its maker's ethnicity, and houses using the same technique instantiate each group's migration pattern (fig. 68). Once you see the patterns of log notching revealed by mapping, you see the migration patterns of the diverse ethnic groups settling the land in the eighteenth and nineteenth centuries. The authors' focus on the links between the material of wood and the specific shaping traditions of craft for each ethnic group allows us to reconstruct various ethnic groups' paths of migration, supplementing the written evidence such as letters, diaries, or genealogical records.

Fig. 68. Map of the distribution of methods of horizontal log construction, which shows the migration paths of various ethnic groups during the eighteenth- and nineteenth-century settlement of the eastern United States. From Fred Kniffen and Henry Glassie, "Building in Wood in the Eastern United States," in *Common Places: Readings in American Vernacular Architecture,* ed. Dell Upton and John Michael Vlach (Athens: Univ. of Georgia Press, 1986), 106, fig. 4.10. Originally published in the *Geographical Review,* copyright © 1966 by the American Geographical Society. Used with permission.

The craft of constructing a house in wood (or other materials) also involves specific skills of carving or otherwise ornamenting building elements and interiors. In investigating eighteenth-century houses in the Chesapeake region, Edward Chappell has used a theory of greater-to-lesser ornament to decode the use of spaces in houses for which there is no written record to give us the identity of rooms.[6] Highly ornamented rooms, he argues, are those in which public reception took place (fig. 69). Kitchens and workrooms typically had no ornament, just simple boards framing the doors and windows. Family rooms such as chambers were ornamented more if they belonged to the master and mistress of the household, while subsidiary bed-rooms for lesser family members or servants had simpler ornamentation or none at all. In the absence of written evidence informing us of the names and uses of rooms in a house, different levels of ornament can be the key to understanding how the several spaces in a house were used.

Materials and ornamentation may also take nontraditional forms in designs of the nineteenth century and later. Imitations of traditional materials were popular in the last two centuries, as Pamela Simpson explains in her study *Cheap, Quick, and Easy—Imitative Architectural Materials, 1870–1930*.[7] She focused her research on materials such as linoleum, rock-faced concrete block, and imitation leather wall coverings. Detractors of imitative materials argued that true craftsmanship was lost when molders and embossers replaced carvers and that clients attempted to step out of their proper social station and imitate their "betters" with the false magnificence attainable through applying imitations to their ceilings, walls, and floors. Clients for the new materials responded that great imitations were beautiful in themselves and that modern imitations of older materials actually improved on the originals in durability, safety, or cleanliness. Simpson was able to uncover nuances of middle-class taste formation and to show how materials became a critical battleground that betrayed class interests.

The scholars discussed above have all worked on issues of building materials, craft, and ornament but have asked different questions and so have brought us different kinds of cultural interpretations. Associating the material of wood and the way it is worked with ethnic traditions gives us maps of immigration and settlement. Inquiring into the way materials are carved and rooms ornamented results in deriving a scheme of possible uses for house spaces not otherwise identified. Observing the popularity of imitation materials and embossed rather than carved ornamental forms offers an unexpected way to clarify aspects of friction among social classes.

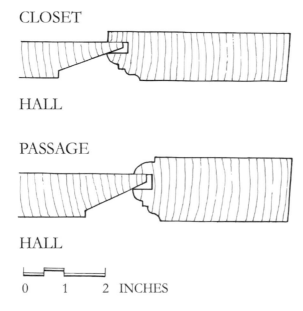

CLOSET

HALL

PASSAGE

HALL

0   1   2   INCHES

Fig. 69. Illustrations contrasting genteel and everyday spaces as indicated by reading molding profiles: the most elaborated moldings are those decorating the hall or other important reception rooms, while the simplest come from less prestigious rooms such as the kitchen, closet and passage. Drawings by Edward Chappell.

Plan and Use

The structure of a building and its finishes show important aspects of a culture's regard for craft, but these reveal nothing about how the specific spaces of that building are used. Let us next look at rooms and their relationships as an analytic lens through which to understand more about human relations. To analyze space and its uses we would obtain or draw plans of all floors of the building under study, ascertain dimensions, describe the rooms and the adjacencies or spatial relationships among rooms, and identify their intended and actual functions. Ideally we would also discover the users' experience of making these rooms work, although that information is hard to come by.

The plans of a typical single-room-occupancy (SRO) hotel provided the starting point for the cultural geographer Paul Groth in his book *Living Downtown*.[8] This building type was common in industrial cities with mobile male labor forces. He found that a particular class of workers—single men employed in maritime trades and construction—preferred the temporary kind of home available by the week in SRO hotels. Corridors lined on both sides with small, one-occupant rooms structured a dwelling suited to transient male workers (fig. 70). While this form of dwelling was often criticized by middle-class reformers and city planners as unsanitary or encouraging shiftless behaviors, Groth found that the SRO hotel served the specific needs of a large urban population who required mobility to meet their occupational needs. The SRO hotel as a building type was nearly erased from the modern urban landscape in the 1970s and 1980s through demolition or renovation, following the dictates of middle-class planners who did not understand the value of these structures. With this demolition, many working-class men were left homeless. By focusing his research on the

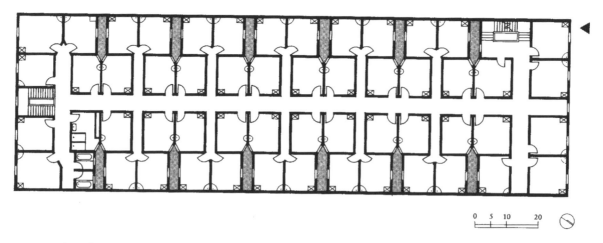

Fig. 70. Plan of a San Francisco single-room-occupancy rooming house used by transient maritime and construction workers. The minimal facilities and small space allotted to each tenant perfectly suited the needs of single men whose work kept them away from home much of the time. From Paul Groth, *Living Downtown: The History of Residential Hotels in the United States* (Berkeley: Univ. of California Press, 1994), 101, fig. 4.10. Copyright © 1994 by The Regents of the University of California. Used by permission of the publisher.

Fig. 71. View inside a typical western North Carolina single-pen house with all functions collected in one main room. From Michael Ann Williams, "The Little 'Big House': The Use and Meaning of the Single-Pen Dwelling," in *Perspectives in Vernacular Architecture II,* ed. Camille Wells (Columbia: Univ. of Missouri Press, 1986), 135. Courtesy of the Great Smoky Mountains National Park.

plan and use of an underexamined building type, Groth was able to explore its spaces and meanings, its critics and its usefulness, and to propose some ways that the SRO hotel as a building type could be revived to improve urban life in the present.

We depend on architectural plans to give us indications of the use of buildings, but different regions may have specific ways of using spaces that plans alone will not reveal. To supplement information conveyed by the plan, the researcher may need to rely on the testimony of users for evidence. In a revealing space analysis, the folklorist Michael Ann Williams looked at Appalachian houses built in a traditional regional manner (fig. 71).[9] By interviewing the longtime residents, Williams ascertained how the rooms in the house were named and how rooms and parts of rooms were used. She found that, counter to more modern houses, the Appalachian houses each had one large room called a "house," which was used for cooking and eating at one end and sleeping at the other end. Instead of separating functions in the dwelling by giving each one a separate room, these residents identified separate uses as customary in different areas of a single large room. Had we imagined that all houses of a period would have spaces that worked in the same way, we would have missed the dramatic differences found from one region to another in American houses, here revealed by interviews with people who used them.

Studying plans and room adjacencies can help us to understand space use to a degree, but the furniture used by households may help us understand more. Furnishings are a key to the use of spaces and may indicate marked ethnic differences in the use of dwellings. The architect Renee Chow analyzed the uses of spaces in San Francisco row houses and nearby suburban houses, and she found evidence of the ways that ethnic groups differently interpret the space of houses.[10] A Hispanic family interpreted their row-house plan to have a central general-purpose room akin to the central patio they had been accustomed to in Mexico. That central room acted as a circulation hub in which people gathered for multiple purposes, as they had on the patio in Mexico. Rooms opening off that central room gained their specific identities by analogy to the Mexican household's uses, rather than from the uses planned by the California developer (fig. 72). In another example, she found that an Asian family interpreted their space as several rooms with the same uses; again the dwelling was inhabited differently

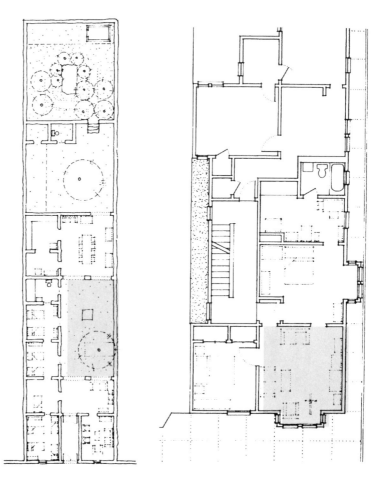

Fig. 72. Mexican tenants in this apartment furnished and used the space as if it were their home in Mexico, creating the equivalent of a central courtyard (A) and circulation space out of the apartment's living room (B). From Renée Chow, *Suburban Space: The Fabric of Dwelling* (Berkeley: Univ. of California Press, 2002), 83. Copyright © 2002 by Renée Chow. Used by permission of the publisher.

A. (left) Mexican house with a courtyard used as circulation hub.

B. (right) San Francisco apartment livingroom used as a hub like the courtyard.

from what was intended by the suburban developer. For the Asian parents and their one child, accustomed to the restricted space of houses in China, each room had a place for play, a place to read or study, and a place for family conversation. Since they preferred to spend time together, this Chinese family all shared a single bedroom, allocating their other bedroom for guests instead of using it as the child's room, as the developer intended. While we might not find much ethnically specific architecture among U.S. houses after World War I in terms of construction methods, materials, and plans, we do find ethnic diversity in the uses of mainstream houses. The vernacular architecture scholar thus can reveal the diverse sensibilities of varied groups of inhabitants within buildings whose superficial space plans are the same.

Scholarship based on building plans that show room relationships have allowed interpretations that range widely. From a study of the single-room-occupancy hotel for single men we gain a new appreciation of a derided type and the rationale for re-creating it in the present. Interviews with inhabitants allow us to supplement the information available on measured plans to expand our knowledge of the uses of interior space in specific regions. The study of rooms and their furniture provides evidence for how different ethnic groups depart from the norm in the ways they use interior spaces.

Artistry and Style

Every building has its own particular external appearance. Its exterior presents an arrangement of forms—voids and solids, symmetrical or not, ornamented or plain—that convey its style. Buildings that are well-developed examples of style typically cost a lot, and their production depends on the needs of elite clients and institutions. The style of a building has always been of concern to traditional architectural historians, and for some, identifying a building's style and describing its nuances may be considered sufficient.

Vernacular architecture scholars would tend to press style information further than this, however, in search of broader cultural meanings. An example is the architectural historian Dell Upton's investigation of early eighteenth-century Virginia houses and churches in his book *Holy Things and Profane*.[11] Upton argues that the exterior and interior stylistic features of wealthy planters' houses and those of churches are similar (figs. 73 and 74). The same architectural details and craftsmanship found in the religious buildings are seen in the secular structures produced by the Virginia elite, but not in the houses of ordinary parishioners. Furthermore these similarities are reinforced by some interior furnishings such as silver cups and trays, called plate. These objects might be executed in a unique mode, proclaiming the planter family's wealth and taste by making visible their access to rarities. Plate from wealthy homes was often donated to churches, there displaying to the parishioners the owners' high standing—and reinforcing the parallels between grand houses and churches by inserting domestic objects into ecclesiastical settings. Upton's searching exploration of style leads him to an interpretation of churches and elite houses as members of the same architectural and cultural system that instilled and reinforced hierarchy in the social life of the Virginia commonwealth. Stylistic similarities between God's houses and planters' houses impressed on lowlier citizens, servants, and slaves the power of elite families. Architectural style, in this analysis, acts as a symbol of the "natural" superiority of Virginia's ruling gentry.

In the category of style, the historic preservationist Catherine Bishir raises a set of questions having to do with race relations. White racial claims to cultural supremacy are explained in Bishir's "Landmarks of Power: Building a Southern Past, 1885–1915."[12] Bishir shows how on their houses elite white families in the post-Reconstruction South used architectural motifs and details that recalled pre–Civil War houses and public buildings. They deployed Ionic porticoes, pediments, and other references to plantation houses and civic buildings of the Anglo-American past, intending to suggest continuity between their present and the great traditions of the colonial and antebellum eras. Shoring up white supremacy was the overt intent of these elites, and they used their architecture to say so: the use of these style features made public their desire to return to a slaveholding "golden age."

The folklorist John Vlach, too, uses style in his analysis of the architecture of slavery; in *Back of the Big House* he recovers the architectural frameworks in which enslaved African Americans lived and worked in the American South.[13] Vlach found that enslaved laborers lived in a wide variety of dwellings, from empty rooms in their masters' basements, attics, or outbuildings, to slave houses constructed for the purpose, to rented rooms in the larger southern towns. During renovations of plantations, masters would sometimes add architectural style features to their slave cabins so that the exteriors matched the new, stylish exteriors of the main house. The resulting ensembles of stylishly

Figs. 73 and 74. Christ Church (fig. 73) and Nelson House (fig. 74) in Virginia both make use of classical architectural elements and brick materials, giving them a similar appearance. Photographs by Elizabeth Cromley.

Figs. 75 and 76. Berkshire Apartments, 1883 (fig. 75) and apartments at 998 Fifth Avenue (fig. 76) reveal a major shift in style from a fragmented and disrupted surface in the 1880s to a smooth classical whole after 1900. Berkshire Apartments from *American Architecture and Building News*, no. 397 (August 4, 1883): n.p; 998 Fifth Avenue from *American Architect* 100, no. 1875 (November 29, 1911): n.p. From the collection of Elizabeth Cromley.

matching main house and outbuildings aggrandized the masters' holdings, while disguising the ways in which slaves on the plantations were deprived of personal choices about their living circumstances. In Bishir's and Vlach's scholarship, architectural style is used as a key to reveal deeper meanings about American race relations encoded in the buildings.

Another example using stylistic analysis to yield cultural information can be found in the architectural historian Elizabeth Cromley's book *Alone Together,* in which she analyzes the styles of New York apartment houses at the turn of the twentieth century.[14] She found that large apartment blocks in the early 1880s typically utilized eclectic architectural styles that were picturesque in outline, full of sculptural incident, with surfaces variegated in color and materials. Twenty years later the characteristic apartment-house style had shifted to a classical vocabulary in which individual architectural details were subsumed under a single unified color and composition (figs. 75 and 76). She showed that this style change, while reflecting a general shift in architectural taste, could also be interpreted as a deeper shift in people's attitudes about living together under one roof. The earlier generation, anxious about losing their privacy and independence by living in an apartment, preferred architectural styles that exaggerated the separate parts of the building as if to stress the many independent families who lived there. By 1900 residents

were more accustomed to and positive about the apartment experience, so they preferred a unified classical style that presented the residents to the public eye as a group
who enjoyed the collective advantages gained by living together. Here an analysis of
style uncovers changing attitudes toward the reciprocal values of privacy and community in urban domestic architecture.

The level of a household's economy and class may also be indicated by stylistic
concerns. Working-class tenement dwellings, largely for immigrants in the 1880s and
1890s, are the subject of historian Lizabeth Cohen's study "Embellishing a Life of
Labor."[15] She traces the argument between immigrant tenement residents and social
workers about the appropriate style and ornament for home furnishings. The social
workers, middle-class women for the most part, urged immigrant housewives to select
simple, unornamented, easily cleaned, arts-and-crafts-style furniture and simplify their
interiors to make them cleaner, healthier, and more American looking. The immigrants, however, chose to import furniture from their home countries and utilize large-
scale beds with elaborate carvings or hangings to help them preserve family rituals and
memories of their mother countries. Cohen's investigation reveals two conflicting
meaning systems embodied in the style and ornament of furnishings and interior decoration, which help us to understand cultural tensions between the middle class and
the working class at the turn of the twentieth century.

Style-based studies have pushed normal understandings of style beyond descriptions of architectural detail to reveal unexpected cultural meanings. The Virginia plantation society guaranteed its hierarchical social relations by reiterating them in the
mirrored stylistic features of elite houses and churches. In their stylistic choices for
building exteriors, apartment dwellers revealed their anxieties about and then their
comfort with living under a shared roof. Working-class tenement dwellers furnished
their domestic spaces with elaborate furniture that challenged the authority of "their
betters," the social workers for whom ornate styles were repugnant.

Cultural Landscapes

Vernacular buildings are often best examined in a context larger than the single work
of architecture. Constellations of several buildings and their immediate surroundings
constitute a landscape that can be analyzed for cultural meanings—meanings that
cannot be uncovered by looking at a single building by itself. The architect Thomas
Hubka has analyzed Maine farmscapes—that is, farmhouses, their outbuildings, and
their immediate landscapes—in *Big House, Little House, Back House, Barn.*[16] Hubka
developed a graphic way to map the uses of farmscape space, focusing on the linking
of outdoor and indoor space usage (fig. 77). The front of the farmhouse, or "big
house," contained the parlor; its immediate outdoor space was the front yard, where
decorative flowers grew. Parlor and front yard worked in concert to convey the gentility of the residents to visitors. The kitchen and domestic work spaces toward the rear
of the farmhouse and in the "little house," a connecting structure, were linked to the
dooryard, where domestic work could continue outdoors. Cooks in the kitchen could

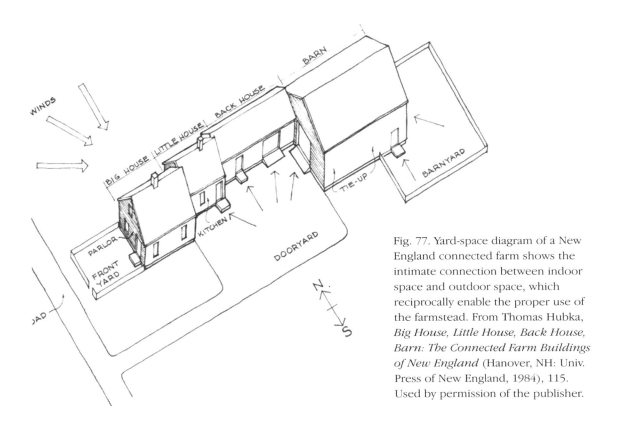

Fig. 77. Yard-space diagram of a New England connected farm shows the intimate connection between indoor space and outdoor space, which reciprocally enable the proper use of the farmstead. From Thomas Hubka, *Big House, Little House, Back House, Barn: The Connected Farm Buildings of New England* (Hanover, NH: Univ. Press of New England, 1984), 115. Used by permission of the publisher.

step outside to feed the chickens in the dooryard. These indoor and outdoor spaces amplified each other's utility. The farmstead continued with a "back house," a work and storage space, and a connected barn, whose interior spaces were likewise supplemented by the farmyard at the back. Hubka's analysis suggests that we must not just look at buildings as independent objects: no interior space can be understood without examining how it functions with its respective outdoor space.

The complex cultural landscape comprised of multiple buildings and the land around them may also change dramatically over time. Tracing generational changes in the immediate landscape of houses in Runnymede, in East Palo Alto, California, the historians Alan Michelson and Katherine Solomonson illuminate the ways that landscape served the inhabitants of successive decades.[17] When first developed in 1916, Runnymede was an agricultural utopia founded to entice well-off suburbanites back to the land. On long and deep one-acre lots, residents deployed houses for themselves, tank houses for water, and chicken coops. From the grid-planned streets, Runnymede looked like other suburban developments with small houses facing modest front yards, but in the back their lots supported agricultural businesses. Chicken farming died out at Runnymede in the 1930s, to be replaced by flower growing. After World War II a subsequent generation of largely Asian residents intensified the floricultural activities of Runnymede, building extended greenhouses on the long, deep lots and producing flowers for the market. Floriculture faded out, and in the 1960s a highway cut through the neighborhood resulted in a divided landscape: on the Runnymede side of East Palo Alto, African American, Latinos, and Pacific Islanders lived in comparative poverty. The area became known as a dangerous center of gangs and drugs. In this same Runnymede landscape, yet another generation reinterpreted their house lots as private enclaves fenced in chain link. Some of the deep Runnymede house lots were consolidated and rebuilt as a cul-de-sac street of high-density suburban houses walled into its own enclave. But other households, still connecting to their immigrant traditions, planted family vegetable gardens and converted agricultural tank houses into living quarters. Michelson and Solomonson show how houses and their immediate landscapes were used to produce incomes for and to shelter residents, and how changing economic opportunities led to radical revisions of the same acreage.

At a larger scale the landscape of land and buildings that interests vernacular architecture scholars might encompass a whole town or even a whole region. *Constructing Townscapes,* by the historian Lisa Tolbert, traces the development of small towns in Tennessee before the Civil War. Tolbert found that in the 1820s and 1830s there was a mixed landscape of houses, commercial structures, and civic buildings all gathered together around town squares. But by the 1850s the town centers were dedicated to commerce and had become refined retail districts, while warehouses and mills clustered around the railroad depots and residential development had removed to neighborhoods (fig. 78). Just as the towns' landscapes were segmented into zones of different uses, so too were the landscapes of individual houses. Each

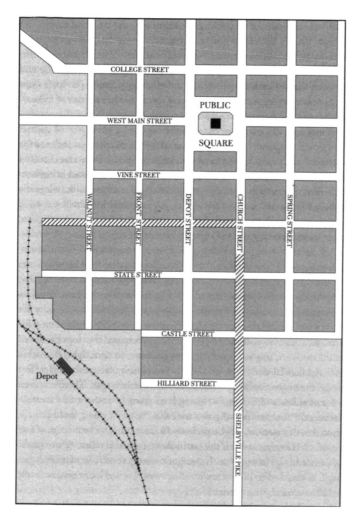

Fig 78. Plan of Murfreesboro, Tennessee, in the 1870s. The consolidation of industry and warehousing near the railroad cleared the way for commercial development around the public square. From Lisa Tolbert, *Constructing Townscapes: Space and Society in Antebellum Tennessee* (Chapel Hill: Univ. of North Carolina Press, 1999), 98. Used by permission of the publisher.

town lot had always contained a house and productive gardens and work spaces. Improvements at midcentury typically encompassed moving work spaces to the rear of the lots and giving the front yards over to genteel ornamental gardens with flowers, gravel walks, and rose bushes. Similarly within the houses the kitchens and food storage spaces were moved to the rear and genteel parlors and reception rooms focused at the front. By looking not just at houses but also at houses within their landscapes, Tolbert illuminates the ways that Tennessee towns were reconceived and restructured to become modern in residents' eyes.[18]

Scholars who extend the study of vernacular architecture to whole landscapes have been able to show the essential interrelation of building spaces to outdoor spaces in farms, suggesting the need to attend to the indoor-outdoor relationships in all buildings. Larger landscapes can metamorphose over generations, completely changing their meanings—as seen in the study of Runnymede, where the landscape served an original economy based in chicken ranching, then another in floriculture, and then a recent one in fenced suburban residential enclaves. When we notice how commercial and manufacturing work spaces are segregated from genteel spaces in the mid-nineteenth-century reconceptualization of townscapes, the ways that the structure of the larger town landscapes mirror the organization of space in the smaller homescapes are revealed.

The preceding glimpses of scholarship in recent vernacular architecture studies show how broad cultural issues can be uncovered, explored, and interpreted through the lens provided by vernacular buildings and landscapes. The checklist of sources at the end of this book provides numerous additional studies that will give other approaches to understanding culture through its buildings.

CHAPTER 5

Invitation to the House on Richmond Avenue in Buffalo

After seeing how a variety of scholars have applied different questions to vernacular architecture, we bring this study to a conclusion by applying all these interpretive strategies to a single building. At the beginning of this guide we showed you a house in Buffalo, New York. It is an anonymously designed two-family house at 299 Richmond Avenue (fig. 79). In the introduction we supplied little beyond an ad hoc description of the house. With some better tools, we said, it would be more readable, make more sense. Now you have an understanding of what those tools are and how to use them. The Buffalo house has been surveyed: it is located within a streetcar district in an area containing many houses like it, built up around the turn of the twentieth century. It has been documented architecturally—with measured drawings and photographs—and historically, with whatever documents we could find recording details of its construction and life span.

The deed to the house gives a construction date of

Fig. 79. View of 299 Richmond Avenue, Buffalo, New York—a double or two-family house from 1906. Photo by Elizabeth Cromley.

1906, and it appears on city atlases after that date; before 1900 atlases show that the land it is on was a large, undivided holding. The first residents documented in the Richmond Avenue house were the Banks family, according to the 1910 federal census. Theodore Banks, a manager at a milling company, lived there with his wife, Daisy, and their two children, Millard and Margery. The census enumerator did not list anyone living in the second apartment of this double house; available evidence shows only four people living at 299 Richmond Avenue. Buffalo city directories might supplement census information, listing the names of heads of households, although unlike in the federal census, listing one's name in business directories was optional. By 1920 the residents at 299 Richmond had changed. Now Joseph Walsh was renting the house and lived there with his wife, Adelaide, their son, Joseph Jr., and his mother, Harriet, as documented in the federal census. The Walshes supplemented their resources by taking in two boarders, William and Letitia Somerville. These boarders may have made use of two finished attic rooms connected to the upper apartment. The second unit in the house was occupied by Edward and Nettie Roehl and their daughter, Alfreda (fig. 80). Thus the same house was home to three generations comprising nine people in three family units. In 1930 the residents were again different, suggesting that the Richmond Avenue neighborhood fostered mobility. Now the house was home to renters Edna and Fred Mitchel. She was a city health

Fig. 80. Exploded diagram of a double house showing the horizontal division between two households. Drawing by Jane Barrett and Collin Tomb. Used by permission of the Western Regional Architecture Program, University of Utah.

FINISHED ROOM IN ATTIC
LINKED TO UPPER UNIT

UPPER UNIT WITH
SMALL PORCH/DECK

LOWER UNIT
WITH PORCH

inspector, while he worked as a mining engineer. Their daughter, Dora J. Metcalf, resided at the same address—the census enumerator did not document whether their daughter lived with them or in the second unit.

Now it is time to build a narrative about this house that can contribute the kinds of understandings mentioned at the outset: how a building can help us see human behavior, see the mundane aspects of ordinary lives, and glimpse the craft and sense of beauty aimed at by ordinary people. The first analytic lens we will apply is the concept of building type. The Buffalo house is a *double* or *two-family* house, a subtype of "house" that informs us about the middle to lower economic level of the people for whom the house was produced. The two-family house type was a common one in Buffalo in the late nineteenth and early twentieth centuries and deceptively appeared to match the American ideal of a single-family freehold (figs. 81 and 82). The house

Fig. 81. First-floor plan of 299 Richmond Avenue as built. Drawing by Jane Barrett and Collin Tomb. Used by permission of the Western Regional Architecture Program, University of Utah.

Fig. 82. Second-floor plan of 299 Richmond Avenue. Drawing by Jane Barrett and Collin Tomb. Used by permission of the Western Regional Architecture Program, University of Utah.

is not, however, for a single family but instead gives opportunities for economical living since double houses allow two households to share the cost of a free-standing dwelling.

The Buffalo house, in addition to being a two-family type, can be further investigated by observing that its ground-floor unit was subdivided around 1940, making it a member of the type "subdivided double" (fig. 83). There was a flurry of activity in subdividing double houses in Buffalo in the early 1940s in order to make room for World War II industrial workers who flooded into the city to help manufacture steel and other war-related supplies. These extra workers needed apartments, and house owners obliged (and made a profit) by creating additional rental units out of existing housing stock. The house at 299 Richmond could be grouped with other subdivided doubles to analyze their locations. The concept of building type is an analytic tool that allows us to group buildings and learn from the aggregate. Were we to map the locations of these newly created apartments in "subdivided doubles," we could see which neighborhoods provided shelter for the expanded working class of the city.

The next analytic category is architectural materials and craft. The Buffalo house is constructed of wood, assembled of dimensioned lumber from a commercial sawmill and fastened together with mass-produced wire nails. Because it is a twentieth-century house, its ornament was made by a commercial millwork shop, not custom-made for this house but available by catalog or at lumber yards. Whether mass-produced or carved for a specific installation, however, ornament acts as a symbolic system that helps direct people's attention to areas of greater and lesser importance in a building. In the Buffalo house the living room is the most richly ornamented area (fig. 84). Wood columns subdivide the space by bracketing the middle of the twenty-five-foot room length, in effect making it into

Fig. 83. First-floor unit at 299 Richmond Avenue subdivided to make two one-bedroom apartments. Drawing by Jane Barrett and Collin Tomb. Used by permission of the Western Regional Architecture Program, University of Utah.

the equivalent of front and back parlors. In the front section there are elaborate moldings around the windows and door, and molded baseboards and cornice. In the rear portion there is a fireplace ornamented with a carved-wood surround and a mirrored and columned overmantel. As the rooms become more family oriented and less public, they have less ornament.

The analysis of plan and room relationships is the next tool for understanding the human relationships encouraged or limited by the building (see plans in figs. 81 and 82). Since the Buffalo house was originally intended for two households, one on each floor, the original plans for the floors were nearly identical. Each apartment had a double parlor at the street front, with the rear parlor lit by a bay window to the south. This double parlor was divided from the dining room by pocket doors. To the rear of the dining room were a buffering butler's pantry and the kitchen. The sequence of rooms in the rear on the south flank—dining room, pantry, kitchen—was paralleled by another sequence of rooms on the north flank: bedroom, bathroom, bedroom, linked by a hall that contained a built-in closet. An additional bedroom opened directly from the dining room.

Fig. 84. Ornamental millwork used in the parlor and dining room of 299 Richmond Avenue. Photo by Patricia L. Bazelon.

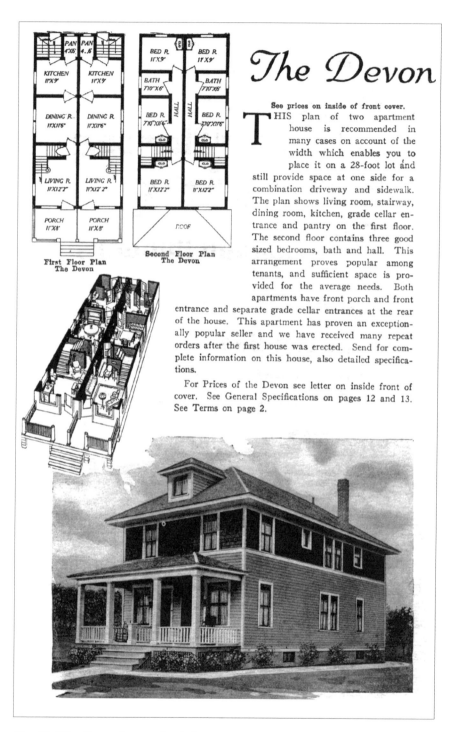

The Devon

See prices on inside of front cover.

THIS plan of two apartment house is recommended in many cases on account of the width which enables you to place it on a 28-foot lot and still provide space at one side for a combination driveway and sidewalk. The plan shows living room, stairway, dining room, kitchen, grade cellar entrance and pantry on the first floor. The second floor contains three good sized bedrooms, bath and hall. This arrangement proves popular among tenants, and sufficient space is provided for the average needs. Both apartments have front porch and front entrance and separate grade cellar entrances at the rear of the house. This apartment has proven an exceptionally popular seller and we have received many repeat orders after the first house was erected. Send for complete information on this house, also detailed specifications.

For Prices of the Devon see letter on inside front of cover. See General Specifications on pages 12 and 13. See Terms on page 2.

Fig. 85. "The Devon," a two-family house variant in which the households were separated by a vertical division rather than on horizontal floors. Plans and specifications were advertised for sale by the Aladdin Co. catalog in 1919.

By studying plan adjacencies and probable uses of rooms, we would gain clues as to how each space in the house served its users; if we could interview the residents or have access to written and photographic records, we would know even more about the specifics of use. Were these uses typical or different from the period norm? Published plans in period magazines or architectural pattern books show that this Richmond Avenue house was common in its plan strategies for organizing a complex set of living demands into a rectangle that could fit on a narrow urban lot. Popular publications such as *Radford's Artistic Bungalows* and *Aladdin Homes* sold plans and specifications, and spread ideas for this type of house around the country (fig. 85).

How do these plans compare with those for a house built a generation earlier or later? Plans from an earlier generation likely would have had spaces less rationalized to nuances of use: the small butler's pantry with its built-in storage cabinets and the built-in fittings in closets belong to an early twentieth-century middle-class sensibility and budget. Further spatial analysis might lead us to an understanding of how a specific ethnic group used domestic space; it might lead us to query how adults and children used spaces differently; or it could be the basis for a gender analysis in which we could observe how domestic space operated differently for the males and females in a household.

In order to determine the use of space in the Richmond Avenue house in recent times, we can make use of interviews with residents. During their tenure from 1982 to 1995, Mr. and Mrs. Ernst found that the room sizes and adjacencies in the Buffalo house easily accommodated changing uses and a changing set of people in residence. The front and back parlors, dining room, and kitchen remained relatively stable in their uses (albeit with changes in furniture), but the four more private, family rooms (one in the attic) enabled frequent shifts in use. For a time Mr. Ernst's son lived in the household, appropriating for his bedroom a room that was later used as a study. Mr. and Mrs. Ernst shared a study at the back of the house for some time and then shifted their desks and libraries to separate rooms. The couple's bedroom was once in a finished attic room; later Mrs. Ernst took that room as her sewing room and the couple moved downstairs to their former shared study, turning it into a bedroom (figs. 86 and 87). Their experience of its flexibility suggests that the changing sets of families using the house in its first three decades may have found it equally accommodating. We could hypothesize that the flexible use of rooms is probably common in late twentieth-century America, due to shifting household demographics and the presence of multiple wage earners, although such a theory flies in the face of architectural programs that specify fixed uses in every space.

If we wanted to inquire into the meaning of exterior style in the Richmond Avenue house, we would start with a detailed description of its elements, including fenestration (types of windows), stairs, porches and similar transitional elements, ornament, and finishes. The house is constructed of wood with clapboard siding on two and a half stories. It has a gable roof with gable ends facing the street and rear yard, and dormer windows on one side. Ornamenting the street facade are wooden classical columns on a front porch that extends across the whole front of the house, and a "Palladian" window in the attic gable (fig. 88). Simple moldings trace the meeting point of walls and roof and mark the window lintels, while vertical boards emphasize the corners of the house. Paint colors pick out some of these details. The repeating fenestration patterns on the ground and second floors confirm that this is a two-family house with the same plan for the upper and lower units. While this house design was widespread, we might expect to find variations in material finishes according to regional preferences. At this house, for example, the basement was constructed of local stone that has a particular grain and color not to be found in other

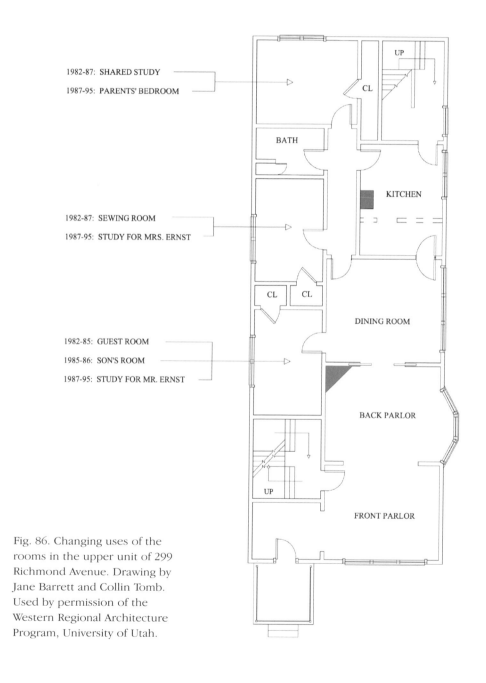

1982-87: SHARED STUDY

1987-95: PARENTS' BEDROOM

CL

UP

BATH

KITCHEN

1982-87: SEWING ROOM

1987-95: STUDY FOR MRS. ERNST

CL   CL

DINING ROOM

1982-85: GUEST ROOM

1985-86: SON'S ROOM

1987-95: STUDY FOR MR. ERNST

BACK PARLOR

UP

FRONT PARLOR

Fig. 86. Changing uses of the rooms in the upper unit of 299 Richmond Avenue. Drawing by Jane Barrett and Collin Tomb. Used by permission of the Western Regional Architecture Program, University of Utah.

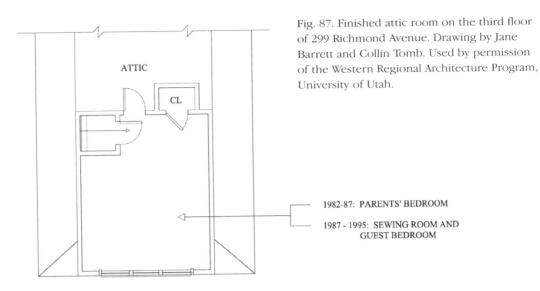

Fig. 87. Finished attic room on the third floor of 299 Richmond Avenue. Drawing by Jane Barrett and Collin Tomb. Used by permission of the Western Regional Architecture Program, University of Utah.

ATTIC

CL

1982-87: PARENTS' BEDROOM

1987 - 1995: SEWING ROOM AND GUEST BEDROOM

regions. The steep roof slope is characteristic of northern climates, and we would expect to find a shallower slope in, say, California.

With a good description of the Buffalo house we could make an assessment of that building's style, show how typical or inventive it was among the stylistic possibilities of its date, and see how its style made it fit into or depart from the familiar styles of its neighborhood and its time period. Because its stylistic features are comprised of minor gestures applied to a simple box, the house does not match examples found in high-style handbooks. The style of this house could be called "street-car-suburb Queen Anne" or perhaps "diluted colonial revival," a vernacular version of some more expensive and stylish houses in adjacent streets in Buffalo and in other parts of the United

Fig. 88. Detail of the third-floor window at 299 Richmond Avenue. Photo by Elizabeth Cromley.

States. We could develop theories of the meaning of its style based on historical refer-
ents: the builders of this house wanted to refer to nearby houses with greater social pre-
tensions but also wanted to sell the house to modest-income buyers. Double-decker
houses of this type often housed parents on the ground floor and a married child on
the second—the double was a type marketed to people who had to stay within a
budget. We might conclude that the reference to fashionable style allowed passersby to
imagine that 299 Richmond was a single-family house, the American ideal, and to gloss
over the fact that this was a shared abode. Our focus on style might result in an evaluation of the aesthetic success or beauty achieved by using this style on this house. Here
we would have to acknowledge that for this middling economic level, the fine craftsmanship found on more costly Queen Anne or colonial revival houses was replaced by
factory-produced architectural details not unique to one house but found throughout
the neighborhood (fig. 89). Thus the owners proclaim, through the style of their house,
that they fit into their neighborhood by adopting stylistic details common to the area,
but they do not claim special attention since theirs is not a unique use of this ornamental vocabulary. Indeed, since details such as theirs are factory-made and available to all,
we could interpret this as a democratic style.

Fig. 89. View of the adjacent houses making up the neighborhood of Richmond Avenue.
Notice the millwork ornament and varied rooflines. Photo by Elizabeth Cromley.

Shifting focus again, let us analyze the Buffalo house not as an individual architectural object but as part of a larger landscape, in order to understand how residential districts in towns are structured. At a medium scale, we can study the house in its lot and consider the outbuildings and landscape features of the immediate home grounds. At a larger scale, we can observe the ways that the house and lot fit into larger patterns of neighborhood, town, and regional landscapes.

If we approached the Richmond Avenue house as a complex of elements occupying the homescape, we could learn more about the set of elements that together sets the immediate context for the house (fig. 90). First, the lot is narrow and deep, giving the house a mere thirty-three feet of street frontage, as is the case with the other houses on its block. Some of the features of the homescape created over time by the families who resided there and used that landscape are the garage and driveway, a clothesline, a vegetable garden, and a flower garden. With this information we can establish comparisons with the homescapes of other houses on the street, in the city, in magazines and pattern books, or in other regions of the country. Mapping the

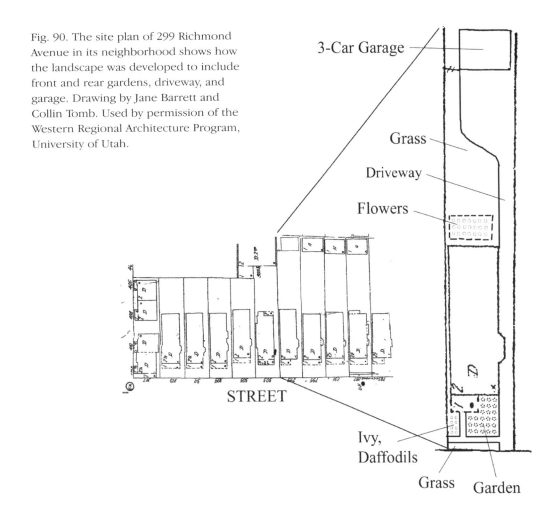

Fig. 90. The site plan of 299 Richmond Avenue in its neighborhood shows how the landscape was developed to include front and rear gardens, driveway, and garage. Drawing by Jane Barrett and Collin Tomb. Used by permission of the Western Regional Architecture Program, University of Utah.

larger contents of the whole site allows us to establish comparisons showing, for example, the role of gardens in cities as compared to suburban development, or to compare the impact of the automobile through the form and location of the garage across several regions, or to see how the suburban homescape compares to its rural cousin, the farmstead, in diverse time periods.

Cultural geographers are interested in mapping the homescape and the relationships of that site to the larger region. To establish the grounds for this kind of analysis, we would describe the Buffalo house's situation in relation to other town institutions—adjacency relations to church, school, shops, workplaces. We would want to ask what resources were available to residents at walking distances compared to driving distances? We would identify public transportation links to the city center and to other towns, and observe the way the town fits into larger geographical and even geological formations. The Buffalo house is located on Richmond Avenue, close to several trolley lines. Developed earlier and electrified in the 1880s and 1890s, trolleys connected largely undeveloped areas of Buffalo to its downtown and spurred a wave of house building in neighborhoods served by the new commuter device. This kind of development in Boston is described in Sam Bass Warner's book *Street-Car Suburbs*.[1] Our analysis of the house in these larger relationships might allow us to make significant observations about how, for example, regional differences in house/town relations create significant transportation and street-pattern changes from one part of the country to another.

The house at 299 Richmond Avenue, Buffalo, has provided a screen on which we have projected several possible interpretive strategies. By analyzing the house as a specific building type—the subdivided Buffalo double—we can use the structure to map the demographic shifts experienced by the city when World War II required a new labor force that needed housing and thereby gain insight into class distribution in Buffalo. If we focus on the building's interior materials and craft, we can understand the Richmond Avenue house as an example of mass-produced millwork applied to the decoration of rooms and observe how these features demarcate the principal reception rooms via elaborate ornament whereas the lesser, private, or service rooms show less ornament. This analysis of ornament's distribution provides connections to the preindustrial usage of ornament as seen in the handcrafted moldings and carvings of eighteenth-century Virginia houses, allowing us to see the longevity of certain architectural principles.

The Richmond Avenue house presents a new face when our analysis turns to plan and room relationships. We observe through firsthand reports on room usage that the most dedicated service rooms and the most ornamented reception rooms tended to keep their use designations, while the remaining rooms had mobile uses and easily accommodated the changes in use required by a family over the span of their inhabitation. When we turn to a stylistic analysis, we find that the house's exterior details can be located within a historicizing vocabulary carried over from the nineteenth century. The widespread use and quality of its mass-produced historical details allow us to interpret the Richmond Avenue house as a statement of democratic values in a city that was home to a large working class. When we apply the broader analytic concerns of understanding a cultural landscape, we place the house within a growing city whose new neighborhoods were connected to the core via trolley lines. Recognizing the house as part of the "streetcar suburb" phenomenon allows us to compare the Buffalo example to houses in similar suburbs near Boston or elsewhere.

The Richmond Avenue house, initially a closed book, now has a wealth of evidence to convey to those who know how to look for and reflect on it. With the same tools you can begin to tell the stories of all sorts of buildings. By assembling the facts about the physical fabric, you discover new information about historic technologies, the building competencies of particular groups of people, and the meanings that craftsmanship carried in other eras. Collecting the available documentation from building records and the like and asking directed questions can open up the buildings you study to yield new views of history. Interpretive strategies such as those discussed above have given us numerous ways to interpret vernacular architecture and "read" it. In each case, by looking at its architecture we learn more about the depth and diversity of American culture than we knew before. We challenge you to use your imagination to move beyond just descriptions of buildings to interpreting the results of your research. Perhaps you will add your own chapters to the ongoing story of vernacular architecture's meanings.

NOTES

INTRODUCTION

1. James Deetz, *Invitation to Archaeology* (Garden City, NY: Natural History Press, 1967).

2. Material culture as a field of academic inquiry is surveyed in Thomas J. Schlereth, ed., *Material Culture: A Research Guide* (Lawrence: Univ. Press of Kansas, 1985); Robert Blair St. George, ed., *Material Life in America, 1600–1860* (Boston: Northeastern Univ. Press, 1988); and Gerald L. Pocius, ed., *Living in a Material World: Canadian and American Approaches to Material Culture* (St. John's, Newfoundland: Institute of Social and Economic Research, 1991).

3. James Deetz, "Material Culture and Archaeology—What's the Difference?" in *Historical Archaeology and the Importance of Material Things,* ed. Leland Ferguson (Columbia, SC: The Society for Historical Archaeology, 1977), 10.

4. The individualistic nature of the American physical environment is specifically treated in James Deetz, *In Small Things Forgotten: The Archaeology of Early American Life* (New York: Anchor Press/Doubleday, 1977). See also Edward Hall, *The Hidden Dimension* (Garden City, NY: Anchor Books, 1969).

5. See Henry Glassie, "Meaningful Things and Appropriate Myths: The Artifact's Place in American Studies," in St. George, *Material Life in America,* 63–94.

6. See Dell Upton, "Form and User: Style, Mode, Fashion, and the Artifact," in Pocius, *Living in a Material World,* 156–57.

7. The textlike quality of buildings is treated in Bernard L. Herman, "The Objects of Discourse," in Pocius, *Living in a Material World,* 3–54; and Bernard L. Herman, *The Stolen House* (Charlottesville: Univ. Press of Virginia, 1992), 3–16.

8. Gabrielle M. Lanier and Bernard L. Herman, *Everyday Architecture of the Mid-Atlantic: Looking at Buildings and Landscapes* (Baltimore: Johns Hopkins Univ. Press, 1997), 1.

9. Cary Carson, "Doing History with Material Culture," in *Material Culture and the Study of American Life,* ed. Ian M. G. Quimby (New York: W. W. Norton, 1978), 45.

10. Clifford Geertz, *The Interpretation of Cultures* (New York: HarperCollins, 1973), 6–30. For the limitations of ethnography, see James Clifford, ed., *Writing Culture: The Poetics and Politics of Ethnography* (Berkeley: Univ. of California Press, 1986).

11. Rhys Isaac, *The Transformation of Virginia, 1740–1790* (Chapel Hill: Univ. of North Carolina Press, 1982), 324. See also his "Ethnographic Method in History: An Action Approach," in St. George, *Material Life in America,* 39–62.

12. Camille Wells, "New Light on Sunnyside: Architectural and Documentary Testaments of an Early Virginia House," *Bulletin of the Northumberland County Historical Society* 32 (1995): 3.

13. Henry Glassie, "A More Human History," chap. 2 in *Folk Housing in Middle Virginia: A Structural Analysis of Historic Artifacts* (Knoxville: Univ. of Tennessee Press, 1975), 8–12.

14. Pierce Lewis, "Axioms for Reading the Landscape," in *The Interpretation of Ordinary Landscapes,* ed. D. W. Meinig (New York: Oxford Univ. Press, 1979), 11–32.

15. See Henry Glassie, "Folk Art," in *Folklore and Folklife: An Introduction,* ed. Richard M. Dorson (Chicago: Univ. of Chicago Press, 1972), 253–80; and Jules David Prown, "Mind in Matter: An Introduction to Material Culture Theory and Method," in St. George, *Material Life in America,* 19–20.

16. See Michael Steinitz, "Rethinking Geographical Approaches to the Common House: The Evidence from Eighteenth-Century Massachusetts," in *Perspectives in Vernacular Architecture III,* ed. Thomas Carter and Bernard Herman (Columbia: Univ. of Missouri Press, 1989), 16–26.

17. M. Gottdiener, *The Social Production of Urban Space,* 2nd ed. (Austin: Univ. of Texas Press, 1994), xv. See also Henri Lefebvre, *The*

Production of Space (Oxford: Blackwell, 1974); Michel de Certeau, *The Practice of Everyday Life* (Berkeley: Univ. of California Press, 1984); and Upton, "Form and User," 161–62.

18. See Robert Sommer, *Personal Space: The Behavioral Basis for Design* (Englewood Cliffs, NJ: Prentice-Hall, 1969); and Hall, *The Hidden Dimension.*

CHAPTER 1

1. David Watkin, *The Rise of Architectural History* (Chicago: Univ. of Chicago Press, 1980).

2. For histories of the Vietnam War era, see Todd Gitlin, *The Sixties: Years of Hope, Days of Rage* (New York, 1987); Allen Matusow, *The Unraveling of America* (New York, 1984); David Farber and Beth Bailey, *The Columbia Guide to America in the 1960s* (New York: Columbia Univ. Press, 2001); and Andrew Hunt, "When Did the Sixties Happen?," *Journal of Social History* (September 1999): 147–61.

3. For a current inquiry into the concept of the everyday, see Dell Upton, "Architecture in Everyday Life," *New Literary History* 33 (Autumn 2002): 707–23.

4. See Dell Upton and John Michael Vlach, eds., *Common Places: Readings in American Vernacular Architecture* (Athens: Univ. of Georgia Press, 1986), xiii–xxiv; Camille Wells, "Old Claims and New Demands," in *Perspectives in Vernacular Architecture, II*, ed. Camille Wells (Columbia: Univ. of Missouri Press, 1986), 1–10; and Thomas Carter and Bernard L. Herman, "Toward a New Architectural History," in *Perspectives in Vernacular Architecture, IV*, ed. Thomas Carter and Bernard Herman (Columbia: Univ. of Missouri Press, 1991), 1–8.

5. A comprehensive history of the vernacular architecture studies movement has yet to be written. The impact of the new architectural history at the state level is treated in Camille Wells, "The Multistoried House: Twentieth-Century Encounters with the Domestic Architecture of Colonial Virginia," *Virginia Magazine of History and Biography* 106 (Autumn 1998): 353–418.

6. See William Rhodes, "The Discovery of America's Architectural Past, 1874–1914," in *The Architec-*

tural Historian in America, ed. Elisabeth Blair MacDougall (Washington, DC: National Gallery of Art, 1990), 23–39; Norman M. Isham and Albert F. Brown, "Early Rhode Island Houses," in Upton and Vlach, *Common Places,* 149–58; Isham and Brown, *Early Rhode Island Houses: An Historical and Architectural Study* (Providence, RI: Preston and Rounds, 1895); and Isham and Brown, *Early Connecticut Houses: An Historical and Architectural Study* (Providence, RI: Preston and Rounds, 1900); and J. Frederick Kelly, *Early Domestic Architec-ture of Connecticut* (New Haven: Yale Univ. Press, 1924).

7. Abbott Lowell Cummings, *Rural Household Inventories, Establishing the Names, Uses and Furnishings of Rooms in the Colonial New England Home, 1675–1775* (Boston: Society for the Preservation of New England Antiquities, 1964); Abbott Lowell Cummings, *The Framed Houses of Massachusetts Bay, 1625–1725* (Cambridge: Harvard Univ. Press, 1979). SPNEA has recently changed its name to Historic New England.

8. Henry Glassie, *Pattern in the Material Folk Culture of the Eastern United States* (Phila-delphia: Univ. of Pennsylvania Press, 1968); Henry Glassie, "The Variation of Concepts within Tradition: Barn Building in Otsego County, New York," in *Man and Cultural Heritage: Papers in Honor of Fred B. Kniffen*, ed. H. J. Walker and W. G. Haag (Baton Rouge: School of Geoscience, Louisiana State Univ., 1974); Henry Glassie, "Folk Art"; Henry Glassie, "Eighteenth-Century Cultural Process in Delaware Valley Folk Building," *Winterthur Portfolio* 7 (1973); and Glassie, *Folk Housing in Middle Virginia.*

9. See John Demos, *A Little Commonwealth: Family Life in Plymouth Colony* (New York: Oxford Univ. Press, 1970); Roger Thompson, *Sex in Middlesex: Popular Mores in a Massachusetts County, 1649–1699* (Amherst: Univ. of Massachusetts Press, 1986); Darrett B. Rutman and Anita H. Rutman, *A Place in Time: Middlesex County, Virginia, 1650–1750* (New York: W. W. Norton, 1984); and Elizabeth Blackmar, *Manhattan for Rent, 1785–1850* (Ithaca, NY: Cornell Univ. Press, 1989).

10. Isaac, *The Transformation of Virginia;* Sally McMurry, *Families and Farmhouses in Nineteenth-Century America* (New York: Oxford Univ. Press, 1988); Robert Blair

St. George, *Conversing by Signs: Poetics of Implication in Colonial New England Culture* (Chapel Hill: Univ. of North Carolina Press, 1998); and Richard Bushman, *The Refinement of America: Persons, Houses, Cities* (New York: Vintage Books, 1993).

11. Robert Stipe, ed., *A Richer Heritage: Historic Preservation in the Twenty-First Century* (Chapel Hill: Univ. of North Carolina Press, 2003); Norman Tyler, *Historic Preservation: An Introduction to Its History, Principles, and Practice* (New York: W. W. Norton, 1999); and William J. Mur tagh, *Keeping Time: The History and Theory of Preservation in America* (Pittstown, NJ: Main Street Press, 1988).

12. A list of these early preservation-inspired studies would be too long, but it is important to point out the work of Catherine Bishir in North Carolina, Bernard Herman in Virginia and Delaware, Orlando Rideout IV in Maryland, Dell Upton and Edward Chappell in Virginia, Camille Wells in Kentucky, and Chris Wilson and Boyd Pratt in New Mexico, to name but a few.

13. John J.-G. Blumenson, *Identifying American Architecture: Pictorial Guide to Styles and Terms* (Nashville, TN: American Association for State and Local History, 1977); John Poppeliers, Allen Chambers, and Nancy B. Schwartz, *What Style Is It? A Guide to American Architecture* (Washington, DC: Preservation Press, 1983).

14. See Carol Rifkind, *A Field Guide to American Architecture* (New York: New American Library, 1980); Thomas Carter and Peter L. Goss, *Utah's Historic Architecture: A Guide* (Salt Lake City: Univ. of Utah Press, 1986); and Virginia McAlester and Lee McAlester, *A Field Guide to American Houses* (New York: Alfred Knopf, 1991).

15. Visit the Vernacular Architecture Forum's Web site: http://www.vernaculararchitectureforum.org/.

16. See Dell Upton, "The Power of Things: Recent Studies in American Vernacular Architecture," in Schlereth, *Material Culture*, 57–78; and Wells, "Old Claims and New Demands," 1–10.

17. Eric Mercer, *English Vernacular Houses: A Study of Traditional Farmhouses and Cottages* (London: Her Majesty's Stationery Office, 1975), 1; Upton and Vlach, *Common Places*, xvi.

18. Bernard Rudofsky, *Architecture without Architects: A Short Introduction to Non-Pedigreed Architecture* (Albuquerque: Univ. of New Mexico Press, 1964).

19. Remember, the most pervasive kinds of extant buildings may or may not be the ones that were common in the past. Architectural examples that survive are often those that have received the most maintenance and that reside in unblighted neighborhoods and were quite exceptional when they were constructed.

20. See Deetz, *In Small Things Forgotten;* Clifford Edward Clark Jr., *The American Family Home, 1800–1960* (Chapel Hill: Univ. of North Carolina Press, 1986); and Anthony King, *The Bungalow: The Production of Global Culture* (London: Routledge and Kegan Paul, 1984).

21. Cary Carson, "Architecture as Social History," unpublished paper delivered at the Vernacular Architecture Forum conference, Williamsburg, Virginia, May 2002.

22. Dell Upton, *America's Architectural Roots: Ethnic Groups That Built America* (Washington, DC: Preservation Press, 1986).

23. See Dell Upton, "Architectural Change in Colonial Rhode Island: The Mott House as a Case Study," *Old-Time New England* 69 (January–June 1979): 18–33; Catherine Bishir, "The Montmorenci–Prospect Hill School: A Study of High-Style Vernacular Architecture in the Roanoke Valley," in *Carolina Dwelling: Towards Preservation of Place; In Celebration of the North Carolina Vernacular Architecture,* ed. Doug Swaim (Raleigh: North Carolina State Univ., 1970), 84–103; Annmarie Adams, "The Eichler Home: Intention and Experience in Postwar Suburbia," in *Gender, Class, and Shelter: Perspectives in Vernacular Architecture,* V, ed. Elizabeth Cromley and Carter Hudgins (Knoxville: Univ. of Tennessee Press, 1995), 164–78.

24. For example, see Gwendolyn Wright, *Building the Dream: A Social History of Housing in America* (New York: Pantheon, 1981); Dolores Hayden, *Seven American Utopias: The Architecture of Communitarian Socialism* (Cambridge: MIT Press, 1981); Henry C. Binford, *The First Suburbs: Residential Communities in the Boston Periphery, 1815–1860* (Chicago: Univ. of Chicago Press, 1985); and Mary Corbin Sies and Christopher Silver, eds., *Planning the*

Twentieth-Century American City (Baltimore: Johns Hopkins Univ. Press, 1996).

25. For cultural landscape studies, see Meinig, *The Interpretation of Ordinary Landscapes;* John Brinckerhoff Jackson, *Discovering the Vernacular Landscape* (New Haven: Yale Univ. Press, 1984); Paul Groth and Todd Bressi, eds., *Understanding Ordinary Landscapes* (New Haven: Yale Univ. Press, 1997); and Chris Wilson and Paul Groth, eds., *Everyday America: Cultural Landscape Studies After J. B. Jackson* (Berkeley: Univ. of California Press, 2003).

26. Victor Burgin, *In/Different Spaces: Place and Memory in Visual Culture* (Berkeley: Univ. of California Press, 1996), 20.

27. George Kubler, *The Shape of Time: Remarks on the History of Things* (New Haven: Yale Univ. Press, 1962), 1.

28. Le Corbusier, *Towards a New Architecture* (1925; reprint edition, New York: Dover, 1986), 72.

29. Nora Pat Small, "New England Farmhouses in the Early Republic: Rhetoric and Reality," in *Shaping Communities: Perspectives in Vernacular Architecture, VI,* ed. Elizabeth Cromley and Carter Hudgins (Knoxville: Univ. of Tennessee Press, 1997), 33–45; Ritchie Garrison, *Landscape and Material Life in Franklin County, Mass., 1770–1860* (Knoxville: Univ. of Tennessee Press, 1991), chap. 7.

30. Claude Lévi-Strauss, *The Savage Mind* (Chicago Press, 1969): 16–22 as cited in Glassie, "Folk Art"; Henry Glassie, "Structure and Function: Folklore and the Artifact," *Semiotica* 7 (1973): 313–51.

31. Thomas Hubka, "Just Folks Designing: Vernacular Designers and the Generation of Form," in Upton and Vlach, *Common Places,* 426–32.

32. Catherine Bishir, "Jacob Holt: An American Builder," in Upton and Vlach, *Common Places,* 447–81.

33. See Elizabeth Cromley, "Modernizing, or 'You Never See a Screen Door on Affluent Homes,'" *Journal of American Culture* 5 (Summer 1982): 71–79; Bernard L. Herman, "Time and Performance: Folk Houses in Delaware," in *American Material Culture and Folklife: A Prologue and Dialogue,* ed. Simon J. Bronner (Ann Arbor: UMI Research Press, 1985),

155–76; and Stewart Brand, *How Buildings Learn: What Happens After They're Built* (New York: Viking, 1994).

34. Elizabeth Cromley, "At Home on Astor Street: Uses of Interior Space at the Charnley House," in *The Charnley House—Louis Sullivan, Frank Lloyd Wright, and the Making of Chicago's Gold Coast,* ed. Richard Longstreth (Chicago: Univ. of Chicago Press, 2004). For an architectural history that collapses the distinctions between high style and vernacular buildings, see Dell Upton, *Architecture in the United States* (New York: Oxford Univ. Press, 1998).

CHAPTER 2

1. Glassie, *Folk Housing in Middle Virginia,* 2.

2. See F. N. McCoy, *Researching and Writing in History: A Practical Handbook for Students* (Berkeley: Univ. of California Press, 1974), 8–20.

3. You may find these maps at your local USGS office (they are located in most major cities), in larger libraries (university libraries generally have extensive holdings of USGS maps), and online through the USGS Web site and companies such as TerraServer.

4. Sanborn fire insurance maps are also available in most university and public libraries, and often may be accessed online by region, state, and city. Most collections now offer guides to interpreting map symbols and describe when changes occurred in the kinds of information presented on the maps. For example, in the 1880s and 1890s Sanborn maps did not show porches, but in the first decades of the twentieth century they did; an unsuspecting researcher therefore might view the porches depicted after 1900 as new additions, though they could be new only to the maps.

5. See Sally Kress Tompkins, "Survey," in *Recording Historic Structures,* ed. John A. Burns (Washington, DC: American Institute of Architects, 1989), 18–45; and *Guidelines for Local Surveys: A Basis for Preservation Planning,* National Register Bulletin 24 (Washington, DC: National Park Service, 1985).

6. See Cary Carson, "Doing History with Material Culture," 48; and Dell Upton, "Architecture in Everyday Life," 707–23.

7. Richard Longstreth, *The Buildings of Main Street: A Guide to American Commercial Architecture* (Washington, DC: Preservation Press, 1987); Glassie, *Pattern in the Material Folk Culture of the Eastern United States;* McAlester and McAlester, *Field Guide to American Houses;* and Rifkind, *A Field Guide to American Architecture.*

8. Edward A. Chappell, "Architectural Recording and the Open-Air Museum: A View from the Field," in Wells, *Perspectives in Vernacular Architecture II*, 24.

9. Ronald W. Brunskill, *Illustrated Handbook of Vernacular Architecture* (London: Faber and Faber, 1971), 27.

10. Jeff Dean*, Architectural Photography: Techniques for Architects, Preservationists, Historians, Photographers, and Urban Planners* (Nashville, TN: American Association for State and Local History, 1981). See also William L. Lebovich, "Photography," in *Recording Historic Structures*, 2nd. ed., ed. John A. Burns (Hoboken, NJ: John Wiley and Sons, 2004), 52–87.

11. See Thomas Hubka and Francis Downing, "Diagramming: A Visual Language," in Wells, *Perspectives in Vernacular Architecture II,* 44–52.

12. For instruction in drawing a building, see Catherine L. Lavoie, "Recording Vernacular Building Forms," in Burns, *Recording Historic Structures*, 2nd. ed., 142–57; and Gabrielle M. Lanier and Bernard L. Herman, "Recording Historic Buildings," chap. 8 in *Everyday Architecture of the Mid-Atlantic,* 316–50.

13. Experience—getting out and looking at many buildings—is the best teacher in learning to read the architectural fabric. A good survey is found in Travis C. McDonald Jr., *Understanding Old Buildings: The Process of Architectural Investigation,* Preservation Briefs 35 (Washington, DC: National Park Service, n.d.).

14. Indispensable readings in this area include Carl R. Lounsbury, *An Illustrated Glossary of Early Southern Architecture and Landscape* (New York: Oxford Univ. Press, 1994); Charles E. Peterson, ed., *Building Early America* (Radnor, PA: Chilton Book Company, 1976); Brooke Hindle, ed., *Material Culture of the Wooden Age* (Tarrytown, NY: Sleepy Hollow Press, 1981); H. Ward Jandl, ed., *The Technology of Historic American Buildings: Studies of the Materials, Craft Processes, and the Mechanization of Building Construction* (Washington, DC: Foundation for Preservation Technology/Association for Preservation Technology, 1983); and Alan Marcus and Howard Segal, *Technology in America: A Brief History* (New York: Harcourt Brace Jovanovich, 1989).

15. See in particular the techniques of discovery outlined in Lanier and Herman, "Construction," chap. 3 in *Everyday Architecture of the Mid-Atlantic*, 61–118.

16. Glassie, *Pattern in the Material Folk Culture of the Eastern United States*; Fred Kniffen and Henry Glassie, "Building in Wood in the Eastern United States: A Time-Place Perspective," in Upton and Vlach, *Common Places,* 159–81; and Warren E. Roberts, "The Tools Used in Building Log Houses in Indiana," in Upton and Vlach, *Common Places,* 182–203.

17. See Lounsbury, *Illustrated Glossary;* Edward Chappell, "Looking at Buildings," in *Fresh Advices: A Research Supplement* (Williamsburg, VA: Colonial Williamsburg Foundation, 1984), i–vi; Herbert Gottfried and Jan Jennings, *American Vernacular Design, 1870–1940: An Illustrated Glossary* (New York: Van Nostrand Reinhold, 1985); and Pamela H. Simpson, *Cheap, Quick, and Easy: Imitative Architectural Materials, 1870–1930* (Knoxville: Univ. of Tennessee Press, 1999).

CHAPTER 3

1. See Glassie, *Pattern in the Material Folk Culture of the Eastern United States,* 78.

2. See Dell Upton, "Early Domestic Vernacular Architecture in Eighteenth-Century Virginia," in Upton and Vlach, *Common Places,* 315–36.

3. A good survey of research methods and techniques is found in Alison K. Hoagland and Gray Fitzsimmons, "History," in Burns, *Recording Historic Structures,* 2nd ed., 26–51.

4. See Talbot Hamblin, *Greek Revival Architecture in America* (New York: Oxford Univ. Press, 1944); Clay Lancaster, *The American Bungalow, 1880–1930* (New York: Abbeville Press, 1985); Dell Upton, "Traditional Timber Framing," in Hindle, *Material Culture of the Wooden Age,*

35–93; and Peter Collins, *Concrete, The Vision of a New Architecture: A Study of Auguste Perret and His Precursors* (London: Faber and Faber, 1959).

5. See Deetz, *In Small Things Forgotten,* 16–18. The opposite system, establishing a "date before which," or *terminus ante quem*, is more difficult, as Deetz notes, "since any number of factors might account for the absence of a given artifact type."

6. See the chapter on construction in Lanier and Herman, *Everyday Architecture of the Mid-Atlantic,* 61–118. Nails are treated specifically in Lee H. Nelson, *Nail Chronology: As an Aid to Dating Old Buildings,* Technical Leaflet 48 (Nashville, TN: American Association for State and Local History, 1968); and Jay D. Edwards and Tom Wells, *Historic Louisiana Nails: Aids to the Dating of Old Buildings,* Fred B. Kniffen Cultural Resources Laboratory Monograph 2 (Baton Rouge: Dept. of Geography and Anthropology, Louisiana State Univ., 1993).

7. An excellent source for information on the land records, prepared for the Association of State and Local History, is Barbara Howe et al., *Houses and Homes: Exploring Their History* (Nashville, TN: American Association for State and Local History, 1987).

8. Deetz, *Invitation to Archaeology,* 37–40; D. W. H. Miles, M. J. Worthington, and Anne Andrus Grady, *Development of Standard Tree-Ring Chronologies for Dating Historic Structures in Eastern Massachusetts* (Boston: Society for the Preservation of New England Antiquities and Great Bay Tree-Ring Laboratory, 2001); Camille Wells, William J. Callahan, and Edward R. Cook, *The Drama of Discovered Origins: Using Dendrochronology to Date Early Virginia Houses* (Charlottesville: Univ. of Virginia School of Architecture, 2002); and Susan L. Buck, "The Aiken-Rhett House: A Comparative Architectural Paint Study" (Ph.D. diss., Univ. of Delaware, 2003).

9. Deetz, *Invitation to Archaeology,* 26–33.

10. See Herman, "Time and Performance," 155–76.

11. See Denis Wood, *The Power of Maps* (New York: Guilford Press, 1992); and Upton, *Architecture in the United States,* 187–246.

12. Edward Soja, *The Political Organization of Space* (Washington, DC: Association of American Geographers, 1971).

13. See William M. Kelso and Rachel Most, eds., *Earth Patterns: Essays in Landscape Archaeology* (Charlottesville: Univ. Press of Virginia, 1990); Donald A. Hutslar, *The Architecture of Migration: Log Construction in the Ohio Country, 1750–1850* (Athens: Ohio Univ. Press, 1986); and James Borchert, *Alley Life in Washington: Family, Community, Religion, and Folklife in the City, 1850–1970* (Urbana: Univ. of Illinois Press, 1980).

14. Susan Saegert, "Masculine Cities, Feminine Suburbs: Polarized Ideas, Contradictory Realities," in *Women and the American City*, ed. Catherine Stimpson, Elsa Dixler, Martha Nelson, and Kathryn Yatrakis (Chicago: Univ. of Chicago Press, 1980), 93–108.

15. Thomas Hubka, *Big House, Little House, Back House, Barn: The Connected Farm Buildings of New England* (Hanover, NH: Univ. Press of New England, 1984), 151.

16. Leslie Kanes Weisman, *Discrimination by Design: A Feminist Critique of the Man-Made Environment* (Urbana: Univ. of Illinois Press, 1992), 23–27, 86–123.

17. Census information is only available seventy years after the date of collection, which means that currently the last year for census data is 1930.

18. This discussion draws on Upton, *Architecture in the United States,* 256–59; Dell Upton, "Form and User: Style, Mode, Fashion, and the Artfact," in Pocius, *Living in a Material World,* 159–61; and Dell Upton, *Holy Things and Profane: Anglican Parish Churches in Colonial Virginia* (Cambridge: MIT Press, 1986), 102–3.

19. Upton, *Architecture in the United States,* 257.

20. Ibid.

21. See ibid., 258.

22. Jules Prown, "Style as Evidence," *Winterthur Portfolio* 15 (Autumn 1980): 198 (emphasis added).

23. See Upton, *Architecture in the United* States, 33–34; and Robert Bocock, *Consumption* (New York: Routledge, 1993).

24. See Bushman, *The Refinement of America.*

25. See Deetz, *Invitation to Archaeology*, 49–52; and Michel Foucault, *The Order of Things: An Archaeology of the Human Sciences* (New York: Vintage Books, 1973).

26. Henry Glassie, "The Types of the Southern Mountain Cabin," in Jan Harold Brunvand, *The Study of American Folklore: An Introduction* (New York: W. W. Norton, 1968), 361–62.

27. Henry Glassie, "Archaeology and Folklore: Common Anxieties, Common Hopes," in *Historical Archaeology and the Importance of Material Things*, Special Publication Series, No. 2, ed. Leland Ferguson (Columbia, SC: Society for Historical Archaeology, 1977), 27.

28. Christian Norberg-Schulz, *Intentions in Architecture* (Cambridge: MIT Press, 1965), 109–30.

29. Kenneth L. Ames, "Meaning in Artifacts: Hall Furnishings in Victorian America," in Upton and Vlach, *Common Places,* 240–60; Lizabeth A. Cohen, "Embellishing a Life of Labor: An Interpretation of the Material Culture of American Working-Class Homes, 1885–1915," in Upton and Vlach, *Common Places,* 261–81.

30. See Abbott Lowell Cummings, "Inside the Massachusetts House," in Upton and Vlach, *Common Places,* 219–39.

31. See Edward Chappell and Julie Richter, "Wealth and Houses in Post-Revolutionary Virginia," in *Exploring Everyday Landscapes: Perspectives in Vernacular Architecture,* VII, ed. Annmarie Adams and Sally McMurry (Knoxville: Univ. of Tennessee Press, 1997), 3–22.

CHAPTER 4

1. Kingston Heath, *The Patina of Place: The Cultural Weathering of a New England Industrial Landscape* (Knoxville: Univ. of Tennessee Press, 2001).

2. Lanier and Herman, *Everyday Architecture of the Mid-Atlantic.*

3. Glassie, *Folk Housing in Middle Virginia;* Henry Glassie, *Passing the Time in Ballymenone: Culture and History of an Ulster Community* (Bloomington: Indiana Univ. Press, 1995).

4. Angel Kwolleck-Folland, *Engendering Business: Men and Women in the Corporate Office, 1870–1930* (Baltimore: Johns Hopkins Univ. Press, 1994), 42, 120.

5. Fred Kniffen and Henry Glassie, "Building in Wood in the Eastern United States: A Time-Place Perspective," in Upton and Vlach, *Common Places,* 159–80.

6. Edward Chappell, "Looking at Buildings." For these principles in application, see restoration of Blandfield, an Essex County, Virginia, house of 1769–72, restored in the 1980s.

7. Simpson, *Cheap, Quick, and Easy.*

8. Paul Groth, *Living Downtown: The History of Residential Hotels in the United States* (Berkeley: Univ. of California Press, 1994).

9. Michael Ann Williams, "The Little 'Big House': The Use and Meaning of the Single-Pen Dwelling," in *Perspectives in Vernacular Architecture II,* ed. Wells, 130–36. See also Williams's book *Homeplace: The Social Use and Meaning of the Folk Dwelling in Southeastern North Carolina* (Athens: Univ. of Georgia Press, 1991).

10. Renee Chow, *Suburban Space: The Fabric of Dwelling* (Berkeley: Univ. of California Press, 2002), 82–85.

11. Upton, *Holy Things and Profane.*

12. Catherine Bishir, "Landmarks of Power: Building a Southern Past, 1885–1915," *Southern Cultures* 1, no. 1 (1993): 5–46.

13. John Michael Vlach, *Back of the Big House: The Architecture of Plantation Slavery* (Chapel Hill: Univ. of North Carolina Press, 1993).

14. Elizabeth Cromley, *Alone Together: A History of New York's Early Apartments* (Ithaca: Cornell Univ. Press, 1990).

15. Lizabeth Cohen, "Embellishing a Life of Labor," in Upton and Vlach, *Common Places,* 261–80.

16. Hubka, *Big House, Little House, Back House, Barn.*

17. Alan Michelson and Katherine Solomonson, "Remnants of a Failed Utopia: Reconstructing Runnymede's Agricultural Landscape," in Cromley and Hudgins, *Shaping Communities,* 3–20.

18. Lisa Tolbert, *Constructing Townscapes* (Chapel Hill: Univ. of North Carolina Press, 1999), 95–99.

CHAPTER 5

1. Sam Bass Warner, *Street-Car Suburbs: The Process of Growth in Boston, 1870–1900* (Cambridge, MA: Harvard Univ. Press, 1962).

CHECKLIST OF SOURCES

The following checklist follows the research method outlined in the preceding chapters. It identifies the basic sources—those you should go to first as you start your research. Some footnote citations are repeated here, though many are not since this listing is intended as an entrance into the material and not a complete bibliography (of the book or the field).

Why Vernacular Architecture?

Developing a rationale for studying the everyday landscape is treated in:

Carson, Cary. "Doing History with Material Culture." In *Material Culture and the Study of American Life*, edited by Ian M. G. Quimby. New York: W. W. Norton, 1978.

———. "Material Culture: The Scholarship Nobody Knows." In *American Material Culture: The Shape of the Field*, edited by Ann Smart Martin and J. Ritchie Garrison. Winterthur, DE: Henry Francis du Pont Winterthur Museum, 1997.

Glassie, Henry. "A More Human History." In Henry Glassie, *Folk Housing in Middle Virginia: A Structural Analysis of Historic Artifacts*, 8–12. Knoxville: University of Tennessee Press, 1975.

Vernacular Architecture and Material Culture

The field of vernacular architecture studies owes much to the larger field of material culture. For an introduction to material culture studies, see the following:

Glassie, Henry. "Meaningful Things and Appropriate Myths: The Artifact's Place in American Studies." In *Material Life in America, 1600–1860*, edited by Robert Blair St. George, 63–92. Boston: Northeastern University Press, 1988.

Prown, Jules. "Mind in Matter: An Introduction to Material Culture Theory and Method." *Winterthur Portfolio* 17, no. 1 (1982): 1–19; reprinted in *Material Life in America, 1600–1860*, edited by Robert Blair St. George, 17–38. Boston: Northeastern University Press, 1988.

Schlereth, Thomas. "Material Culture and Cultural Research." In *Material Culture: A Research Guide*, edited by Thomas Schlereth, 1–34. Lawrence: University Press of Kansas, 1985.

Vernacular Architecture Definitions

Carter, Thomas, and Bernard L. Herman. "Toward a New Architectural History." In *Perspectives in Vernacular Architecture IV*, edited by Thomas Carter and Bernard L. Herman, 1–8. Columbia: University of Missouri Press, 1991.

Glassie, Henry. *Vernacular Architecture*, 17–21. Bloomington: University of Indiana Press, 2000.

Hubka, Thomas. "American Vernacular Architecture." In *Advances in Environment, Behavior, and Design*, vol. 3, edited by E. H. Zube and G. T. Moore, 153–86. New York: Plenum Press, 1990.

Upton, Dell. "The Power of Things: Recent Studies in American Vernacular Architecture." In *Material Culture: A Research Guide*, edited by Thomas Schlereth, 57–78. Lawrence: University Press of Kansas, 1985.

Upton, Dell, and John Michael Vlach. "Introduction." In *Common Places: Readings in American Vernacular Architecture*, edited by Dell Upton and John Michael Vlach, xv–xvii. Athens: University of Georgia Press, 1986.

Wells, Camille. "Old Claims and New Demands." In *Perspectives in Vernacular Architecture II*, edited by Camille Wells, 1–11. Columbia: University of Missouri Press, 1986.

Cultural Landscape Definitions

Architecture exists within the larger human environment—natural and manmade—called a "cultural landscape." For introductory treatments of cultural landscapes, see:

Groth, Paul. "Frameworks for Cultural Landscape Study." In *Understanding Ordinary Landscapes*, edited by Paul Groth and Todd Bressi, 1–24. New Haven: Yale University Press, 1997.

Groth, Paul, and Chris Wilson. "The Polyphony of Cultural Landscape Study." In *Everyday America: Cultural Landscape Studies After J. B. Jackson*, edited by Chris Wilson and Paul Groth, 1–22. Berkeley: University of California Press, 2003.

Lewis, Pierce. "Learning from Looking: Geographic and Other Writing about the American Landscape." In *Material Culture: A Research Guide*, edited by Thomas Schlereth, 35–56. Lawrence: University Press of Kansas, 1985.

Meinig, D. W., ed. *The Interpretation of Ordinary Landscapes*. New York: Oxford University Press, 1979.

Zube, Ervin H., ed. *Landscapes: Selected Writings of J. B. Jackson*. Amherst: University of Massachusetts Press, 1970.

Vernacular Design Process

Understanding vernacular architecture means also confronting the issue of design—how ordinary buildings are conceived and executed.

Bishir, Catherine, Charlotte V. Brown, Carl R. Lounsbury, and Ernest H. Wood III. *Architects and Builders in North Carolina: A History of the Practice of Building.* Chapel Hill: University of North Carolina Press, 1990.

Glassie, Henry. "Folk Art." In *Folklore and Folklife: An Introduction*, edited by Richard M. Dorson, 253–80. Chicago: University of Chicago Press, 1972.

Glassie, Henry. "The Mechanics of Structural Innovation." In Henry Glassie, *Folk Housing in Middle Virginia: A Structural Analysis of Historic Artifacts*, 66–112. Knoxville: University of Tennessee Press, 1975.

Glassie, Henry. "The Variation of Concepts within Tradition: Barn Building in Otsego County, New York." In *Man and Cultural Heritage: Papers in Honor of Fred B. Kniffen*, edited by H. J. Walker and W. G. Haag, 177–235. Baton Rouge: School of Geoscience, Louisiana State University, 1974.

Hubka, Thomas. "Just Folks Designing: Vernacular Designers and the Generation of Form." In *Common Places: Readings in American Vernacular Architecture*, edited by Dell Upton and John Michael Vlach, 426–32. Athens: University of Georgia Press, 1986.

Upton, Dell. "Vernacular Domestic Architecture in Eighteenth Century Virginia." In *Common Places: Readings in American Vernacular Architecture*, edited by Dell Upton and John Michael Vlach, 315–35. Athens: University of Georgia Press, 1986.

Influence of Printed Media on Vernacular Architecture

By the middle years of the nineteenth century, books and magazines on architectural design and taste proliferated throughout the country. The impact of this material on the vernacular tradition is explored in, among others, the following works:

Bishir, Catherine. "Jacob Holt: An American Builder." In *Common Places: Readings in American Vernacular Architecture*, edited by Dell Upton and John Michael Vlach, 447–81. Athens: University of Georgia Press, 1986.

Carter, Thomas. "Folk Design in an Industrial Age: Vernacular Domestic Architecture in Victorian Utah." *Journal of American Folklore* 104 (Fall 1991): 419–42.

Peiff, Daniel D. *Houses from Books: Treatises, Pattern Books, and Catalogs in American Architecture, 1738–1950: A History and Guide.* University Park: Pennsylvania State University Press, 2000.

Upton, Dell. "Pattern Books and Professionalism: Aspects of the Transformation of Domestic Architecture in America, 1800–1860." *Winterthur Portfolio* 19 (Summer/Autumn 1984): 107–50.

Building and Rebuilding

Remodeling is an important part of vernacular architecture research, and the implications of such rebuilding are introduced in the following:

Brand, Stewart. *How Buildings Learn: What Happens After They're Built*. New York: Viking, 1994.

Carter, Thomas, ed. Special "Remodelings" issue of the journal *Material Culture* 19 (Summer–Fall 1987), includes Gerald L. Pocius, "Raised Roofs and High Hopes: Rebuildings on Newfoundland's Southern Shore"; Bernard L. Herman, "Architectural Renewal and the Maintenance of Customary Relationships"; Michael Ann Williams, "'Homeplace': Abandonment, Alteration, and Its Multiple Purposes"; Thomas Carter, "'It Was in the Way, So We Took It Out': Remodeling as Social Commentary"; and Elizabeth Mosby Adler, "Personality and Conformity in Expansion Architecture."

Cromley, Elizabeth. "Modernizing, or, 'You Never See a Screen Door on Affluent Homes.'" *Journal of American Culture* 5 (Summer 1982): 71–79.

Herman, Bernard L. "Time and Performance: Folk Houses in Delaware." In *American Material Culture and Folklife: A Prologue and Dialogue*, edited by Simon J. Bronner, 155–76. Ann Arbor: UMI Research Press, 1985.

Read, Alice Gray. "Making a House a Home in a Philadelphia Neighborhood." In *Perspectives in Vernacular Architecture II*, edited by Camille Wells, 192–99. Columbia: University of Missouri Press, 1986.

Field Survey Techniques and Documentation Methods

Chappell, Edward A. "Architectural Recording and the Open-Air Museum: A View from the Field." in *Perspectives in Vernacular Architecture II*, edited by Camille Wells, 24–36. Columbia: University of Missouri Press, 1986.

Chitham, Robert. *Measured Drawings for Architects*. London: Architectural Press, 1980.

Delyser, Dydia, and Paul F. Starrs. "Doing Fieldwork." Special issue of *Geographical Review* 92 (January–April 2001).

Glassie, Henry. "A Prologue to Analysis." In Henry Glassie, *Folk Housing in Middle Virginia: A Structural Analysis of Historic Artifacts*, 13–18. Knoxville: University of Tennessee Press, 1975.

Guidelines for Local Surveys: A Basis for Preservation Planning. National Register Bulletin 24: Technical Information on Comprehensive Planning, Survey of Cultural Resources, and Registration in the National Register of Historic Places. Washington, DC: National Park Service, 1985.

Lavoie, Catherine L. "Recording Vernacular Building Forms." In *Recording Historic Structures*, 2nd ed., edited by John A. Burns, 142–57. Hoboken, NJ: John Wiley & Sons, 2004.

McDonald, Travis C., Jr. *Understanding Old Buildings: The Process of Architectural Investigation*. Preservation Briefs 35. Washington, DC: National Park Service, n.d.

Lanier, Gabrielle M., and Bernard L. Herman. "Recording Historic Buildings." In Gabrielle M. Lanier and Bernard L. Herman, *Everyday Architecture of the Mid-Atlantic: Looking at Buildings and Landscapes*, 316–50. Baltimore: Johns Hopkins University Press, 1997.

Note: The Library of Congress makes available online the vast archive of measured drawings and photographs of American buildings created under the auspices of the Historic American Buildings Survey, beginning in the 1930s. These are supplemented by drawings made for the Historic American Engineering Record. http://memory.loc.gov/ammem/hhhtml/hhhome.html.

Archival Documentation Methods

Cummings, Abbott Lowell. "Inside the Massachusetts House." In *Common Places: Readings in American Vernacular Architecture*, edited by Dell Upton and John Michael Vlach, 219–39. Athens: University of Georgia Press, 1986.

Hoagland, Alison K., and Gray Fitzsimons. "History." In *Recording Historic Structures*, 2nd ed., edited by John A. Burns, 26–51. Hoboken, NJ: John Wiley and Sons, 2003.

Howe, Barbara J., et al. "Written Records." In Barbara J. Howe et al., *Houses and Homes: Exploring Their History*, 39–58. Walnut Creek, CA: Altamira Press, 1987.

MacFarlane, Alan. *Reconstructing Historical Communities*. London: Cambridge University Press, 1977.

McMurray, Sally. *Families and Farmhouses in Nineteenth-Century America*. New York: Oxford University Press, 1988.

Ethnographic Methods

Bartis, Peter. *Folklife and Fieldwork: A Layman's Introduction to Field Techniques*. Washington, DC: American Folklife Center, 1979.

Glassie, Henry. "Folkloristic Study of the American Artifact: Objects and Objectives." In *Handbook of American Folklore*, edited by Richard M. Dorson, 376–83. Bloomington: Indiana University Press, 1983.

Pocius, Gerald L. *A Place to Belong: Community Order and Everyday Space in Calvert, Newfoundland*. Athens: University of Georgia Press, 1991.

Sitton, Thad, George L. Mehaffy, and O. L. Davis Jr. *Oral History: A Guide for Teachers (and Others)*. Austin: University of Texas Press, 1983.

Williams, Michael Ann. *Homeplace: The Social Use and Meaning of the Folk Dwelling in Southeastern North Carolina*. Athens: University of Georgia Press, 1991.

Photographic Methods

Dean, Jeff. *Architectural Photography: Techniques for Architects, Preservationists, Historians, Photographers, and Urban Planners*. Nashville, TN: American Association for State and Local History, 1981.

Lebovich, William L. "Photography." In *Recording Historic Structures,* 2nd ed., edited by John A. Burns, 52–87. Hoboken, NJ: John Wiley and Sons, 2003.

Dating Techniques

Deetz, James. "Dating." In James Deetz, *Invitation to Archaeology*, 23–42. Garden City, NY: Natural History Press, 1967.

Garvin, James L. "How to Date a Building: The Evolution of Key Features." In James L. Garvin, *A Building History of Northern New England*, 136–73. Hanover, NH: University Press of New England, 2002.

Mapping Strategies

Glassie, Henry. *Pattern in the Material Folk Culture of the Eastern United States*. Philadelphia: University of Pennsylvania Press, 1968.

Kniffen, Fred. "Folk Housing: Key to Diffusion." In *Common Places: Readings in American Vernacular Architecture*, edited by Dell Upton and John Michael Vlach, 3–36. Athens: University of Georgia Press, 1986.

Wood, Denis. *The Power of Maps*. New York: Guilford Press, 1992.

Zelinsky, Wilbur. *The Cultural Geography of the United States*. Englewood Cliffs, NJ: Prentice-Hall, 1973.

Architectural Terminology

Brunskill, R. W. *Illustrated Handbook of Vernacular Architecture*. London: Faber and Faber, 1971.

Forty, Adrian. *Words and Buildings*. New York: Thames and Hudson, 2000.

Harris, Cyril M. *Illustrated Dictionary of Historic Architecture*. New York: Dover Publications, 1977.

Lounsbury, Carl. *An Illustrated Glossary of Early Southern Architecture and Landscape*. New York: Oxford University Press, 1994.

Typologies

Ford, James A. "The Type Concept Revisited." In *Man's Imprint from the Past: Readings in the Methods of Archaeology*, edited by James Deetz, 58–72. Boston: Little, Brown, 1971. Ford's article is one of several in this volume that address taxonomic processes and concerns in artifactual analysis.

Baker, John Milnes. *American House Styles: A Concise Guide*. New York: W. W. Norton, 1994.

Carter, Thomas, and Peter L. Goss, *Utah's Historic Architecture: A Guide* (Salt Lake City: University of Utah Press, 1986).

Glassie, Henry. "The Architectural Competence" and "Counting Houses." In *Folk Housing in Middle Virginia: A Structural Analysis of Historic Artifacts*, 19–65. Knoxville: University of Tennessee Press, 1975.

Gowans, Alan. *Styles and Types of North American Architecture: Social Function and Cultural Expression*. New York: HarperCollins, 1992.

Longstreth, Richard. *The Buildings of Main Street: A Guide to American Commercial Architecture*. Washington, DC: Preservation Press, 1987.

McAlester, Virginia, and Lee McAlester. *A Field Guide to American Houses*. New York: Alfred Knopf, 2000.

Rifkind, Carol. *A Field Guide to American Architecture*. New York: New American Library, 1980.

Studies of Specific Building Types

Cromley, Elizabeth C. *Alone Together: A History of New York's Early Apartments*. Ithaca, NY: Cornell University Press, 1990.

Glassie, Henry. "The Types of the Southern Mountain Cabin." In Jan Harold Brunvand, *The Study of American Folklore: An Introduction*, 338–70. New York: W. W. Norton, 1968.

Groth, Paul. *Living Downtown: The History of Residential Hotels in the United States*. Berkeley: University of California Press, 1994.

Hayward, Mary Ellen, and Charles Belfoure. *The Baltimore Rowhouse*. New York: Princeton Architectural Press, 2001.

Hoagland, Alison K. *Army Architecture in the American West: Forts Laramie, Bridger, and D. A. Russell, 1849–1912*. Norman: University of Oklahoma Press, 2004.

Hubka, Thomas. *Big House, Little House, Back House, Barn: The Connected Farm Buildings of New England*. Hanover, NH: University Press of New England, 1984.

Lancaster, Clay. "The American Bungalow." In *Common Places: Readings in American Vernacular Architecture*, edited by Dell Upton and John Michael Vlach, 76–106. Athens: University of Georgia Press, 1986.

Upton, Dell. *Holy Things and Profane: Anglican Parish Churches in Colonial Virginia*. Cambridge: MIT Press, 1986.

Vlach, John Michael. *Barns*. New York: W. W. Norton, 2003.

———. "The Shotgun House: An African Architectural Legacy." In *Readings in American Vernacular Architecture*, edited by Dell Upton and John Michael Vlach, 58–78. Athens: University of Georgia Press, 1986.

Wallis, Allan D. *Wheel Estate: The Rise and Decline of Mobile Homes*. Baltimore: Johns Hopkins University Press, 1971.

Studies of Cultural Landscapes

Cultural landscape studies consider the shaping of nature in combination with the design and function of buildings; the following works include British and American landscapes:

Blackmar, Elizabeth. *Manhattan for Rent, 1785–1850*. Ithaca, NY: Cornell University Press, 1989.

Borchert, James. *Alley Life in Washington: Family, Community, Religion, and Folklife in the City, 1850–1970*. Urbana: University of Illinois Press, 1980.

Chow, Renee. *Suburban Space: The Fabric of Dwelling*. Berkeley: University of California Press, 2002.

Glassie, Henry. *Passing the Time in Ballymenone: Culture and History of an Ulster Community*. Bloomington: Indiana University Press, 1995.

Heath, Kingston. *The Patina of Place: The Cultural Weathering of a New England Industrial Landscape*. Knoxville: University of Tennessee Press, 2001.

Hoskins, W. G. *The Making of the English Landscape*. London: Hodder and Stoughton, 1955.

Tolbert, Lisa. *Constructing Townscapes*. Chapel Hill: University of North Carolina Press, 1999.

Upton, Dell. "Another City: The Urban Cultural Landscape in the Early Republic." In *Everyday Life in the Early Republic*, edited by Catherine E. Hutchins. Winterthur, DE: Henry Francis du Pont Winterthur Museum, 1994.

Style

Conkey, Margaret, and Christine Hastorf, eds. *The Uses of Style in Archaeology*. Cambridge: Cambridge University Press, 1990.

Garvin, James L. "Why a Building Looks the Way It Does: The Evolution of Style." Chapter 2 in *A Building History of Northern New England*, 95–135. Hanover, NH: University Press of New England, 2002.

Prown, Jules. "Style as Evidence." *Winterthur Portfolio* 15 (1980): 197–210.

Shapiro, Meyer. "Style." In *Anthropology Today: An Encyclopedic Inventory*, edited by A. L. Kroeber. Chicago: University of Chicago Press, 1953).

Upton, Dell. *Architecture in the United States*. New York: Oxford University Press, 1998. See esp. 256–62. Upton explores the subtleties of architecture style in this and the works cited below.

———. "Form and User: Style, Mode, Fashion, and the Artifact." In *Living in a Material World: Canadian and American Approaches to Material Culture*, ed. Gerald Pocius, 156–72. St. John's: Memorial University of Newfoundland, 1991.

———. *Holy Things and Profane: Anglican Parish Churches in Colonial Virginia*. Cambridge, Massachusetts: The MIT Press, 1986. See esp. 101–73

Function

Ames, Kenneth L. *Beyond Necessity: Art in the Folk Tradition.* Winterthur, DE: The Henry Francis de Pont Winterthur Museum, 1977.

Norberg-Shulz, Christian. *Intentions in Architecture.* Cambridge, MA: MIT Press, 1965).

Rapoport, Amos. *House Form and Culture.* Englewood Cliffs, NJ: Prentice-Hall, 1969.

Construction and Materials Technologies

Garvin, James L. "How a House is Built: The Evolution of Building Technology." Chapter 1 in *A Building History of Northern New England*, 5–94. Hanover, NH: University Press of New England, 2002.

Gordon, Robert B., and Patrick M. Malone. *The Texture of Industry: An Archaeological View of the Industrialization of North America.* New York: Oxford University Press, 1994.

Jandl, H. Ward, ed. *The Technology of Historic American Buildings,* Washington, D.C.: Foundation for Preservation Technology/Association for Preservation Technology, 1983.

Kniffen, Fred, and Henry Glassie. "Folk Housing: Key to Diffusion." In *Common Places: Readings in American Vernacular Architecture*, edited by Dell Upton and John Michael Vlach, 3–36. Athens: University of Georgia Press, 1986.

Lanier, Gabrielle, and Bernard Herman. "Construction: Underpinnings, Walling, and Roofing." In *Everyday Architecture of the Mid-Atlantic: Looking at Buildings and Landscapes*, 61–118. Baltimore: Johns Hopkins University Press, 1997.

Marcus, Alan I., and Howard P. Segal. *Technology in America: A Brief History.* New York: Harcourt Brace Jovanovich, 1989.

Simpson, Pamela H. *Cheap, Quick, and Easy: Imitative Architectural Materials, 1870–1930.* Knoxville: University of Tennessee Press, 1999.

Upton, Dell. "Traditional Timber Framing." In *America's Wooden Age: Aspects of its Early Technology*, edited by Brooke Hindle, 51–68. Tarrytown, NY: Sleepy Hollow Restorations, 1975.

Individual Building Studies

Adams, Annmarie. "The Eichler Home: Intention and Experience in Postwar Suburbia." In *Gender, Class, and Shelter: Perspectives in Vernacular Architecture V,* edited by Elizabeth Collins Cromley and Carter L. Hudgins, 164–78. Knoxville: University of Tennessee Press, 1995.

Buchanan, Paul. *Stratford Hall and Other Architectural Studies.* Stratford, VA: Robert E. Lee Memorial Association, Inc., 1998

Lounsbury, Carl. *From Statehouse to Courthouse: An Architectural History of South Carolina's Capitol and Charleston County Courthouse.* Columbia: University of South Carolina Press, 2001.

Ridout, Orlando , V. *Building the Octagon.* Washington, DC: American Institute of Architects Press, 1989.

Upton, Dell. "Architectural Change in Colonial Rhode Island: The Mott House as a Case Study." *Old-Time New England* 69 (Jan–June 1979): 18–33.

Community Case Studies

Candee, Richard M. *Atlantic Heights: A World War I Shipbuilder's Community.* Portsmouth, NH: Portsmouth Marine Society, 1985.

Garrison, J. Ritchie. *Landscape and Material Life in Franklin County, Massachusetts 1770–1860.* Knoxville: University of Tennessee Press,1991.

Herman, Bernard L. *Architecture and Rural Life in Central Delaware, 1700–1900 .* Knoxville: University of Tennessee Press, 1987.

Longstreth, Richard. *City Center to Regional Mall: Architecture, the Automobile, and Retailing in Los Angeles, 1920–1950.* Cambridge, MA: MIT Press, 1997.

Marshall, Howard Wight. *Paradise Valley, Nevada: The People and Buildings of an American Place.* Tucson: The University of Arizona Press, 1995.

Martin, Charles E. *Hollybush: Folk Building and Social Change in an Appalachian Community.* Knoxville: University of Tennessee Press, 1984.

Upton, Dell. "Inventing the Metropolis: Civilization and Urbanity in Antebellum New York." In *Art and the Empire City: New York, 1825–1861*, edited by Catherine Hoover Voorsanger and John K. Howat, 3–46. New York: Metropolitan Museum of Art, 2000.

Regional Studies

Here are a number of works, in addition to those previously mentioned, that take particular regions as their study areas. In this group are several U.S. regions—New England, the Mid-Atlantic, the South, the Great Plains, the Midwest, and the Southwest. Students should also look for works on their own regions in local libraries.

Bunting, Banbridge. *Early Architecture in New Mexico.* Albuquerque: University of New Mexico Press, 1976.

————. *Of Earth and Timber Made: New Mexico Architecture.* Albuquerque: University of New Mexico Press, 1976.

Carson, Cary, Norman F. Barka, William M. Kelso, Garry Wheeler Stone, and Dell Upton. "Impermanent Architecture in the Southern American Colonies." In *Material Life in America*, edited by Robert Blair St. George, 17–38. Boston: Northeastern University Press, 1988.

Eckert, Kathryn Bishop. *The Sandstone Architecture of the Lake Superior Region.* Detroit, Michigan: Wayne State University Press, 2000.

Fairbanks, Jonathan L., and Robert F. Trent, eds. *New England Begins: The Seventeenth Century.* 3 vols. Boston: Museum of Fine Arts, 1982.

Hamilton, Charles M. *Nineteenth-Century Mormon Architecture and City Planning.* New York: Oxford University Press, 1995.

Koop, Michael, and Stephen Ludwig. *German-Russian Folk Architecture in Southeastern South Dakota.* Vermillion, SD: State Historical Preservation Center, 1984.

Markovich, Nicholas C., Wolfgang F. E. Preiser, and Fred G. Sturm, eds. *Pueblo Style and Regional Architecture.* New York: Van Nostrand Reinhold, 1990.

Marshall, Howard Wight. *Folk Architecture in Little Dixie: A Regional Culture in Missouri.* Columbia: University of Missouri Press, 1981.

Peterson, Fred W. *Homes in the Heartland: Balloon Frame Farmhouses of the Upper Midwest, 1850–1920.* Lawrence: University Press of Kansas, 1992.

Roberts, Warren E. *Log Buildings of Southern Indiana.* Bloomington, IN: The Trickster Press, 1984.

Swaim, Doug, ed. *Carolina Dwelling: Towards Preservation of Place; In Celebration of the North Carolina Vernacular Landscape.* Raleigh: North Carolina State University, 1978.

Swank, Scott T. "The Architectural Landscape." In *Arts of the Pennsylvania Germans,* edited by Scott T. Swank, 20–34. New York: W. W. Norton, 1983.

Stine, Linda F., Martha Zierden, Lesley M. Crucker, and Christopher Judge, eds. *Carolina's Historical Landscapes: Archaeological Perspectives.* Knoxville: The University of Tennessee Press, 1997.

van Ravensway, Charles. *The Arts and Architecture of German Settlements in Missouri: A Survey of a Vanishing Culture.* Columbia: University of Missouri Press, 1977.

Ward, Gerald W. R., and William N. Hosley, Jr., eds. *The Great River: Art and Society of the Connecticut Valley, 1635–1820.* Hartford, CT: Wadsworth Atheneum, 1985.

Wilson, Chris. *The Myth of Santa Fe: Creating a Modern Regional Tradition.* Albuquerque: University of New Mexico Press, 1997.

Note also the many state and city guidebooks to architecture, such as those sponsored by the American Institute of Architects, as well as the Buildings of the United States series, published by the Society of Architectural Historians and Oxford University Press.

National and International Studies

Bushman, Richard L. *The Refinement of America: Persons, Houses, Cities.* New York: Vintage Books, 1993.

Carson, Cary, Ronald Hoffman, and Peter J. Albert. *Of Consuming Interests: The Style of Life in the Eighteenth Century.* Charlottesville: The University Press of Virginia, 1994.

Clark, Clifford Edward, Jr. *The American Family Home: 1800–1960.* Chapel Hill: University of North Carolina Press, 1986.

Deetz, James. *In Small Things Forgotten: The Archaeology of Early American Life.* Garden City, New York: Anchor Press/Doubleday, 1977.

King, Anthony. *The Bungalow: the Production of Global Culture.* New York: Oxford
    University Press, 1995.

Loeb, Carolyn S. *Entrepreneurial Vernacular: Developers' Subdivisions in the 1920s.*
    Baltimore: The Johns Hopkins University Press, 2001.

The Need for Theory

Hodder, Ian. *Theory and Practice in Archaeology.* 1992. Reprint, New York: Routledge,
    1995.

Johnson, Matthew. *Archaeological Theory: An Introduction.* Oxford, U.K.: Blackwell, 1999.

Theory in Vernacular Architecture

Dell Upton, in his article "The Power of Things: Recent Studies in American Vernacular
Architecture" (in *Material Culture: A Research Guide*, edited by Thomas J. Schlereth
Lawrence: The University Press of Kansas, 1985, 57–78), categorizes general theoretical approaches to vernacular architecture study as the following: object-oriented studies, social studies, cultural studies, and symbolic studies. The following sources are
organized under those categories.

OBJECT ORIENTED

Cummings, Abbott Lowell. *The Framed Houses of Massachusetts Bay, 1625–1725.*
    Cambridge, MA: Harvard University Press, 1979.

Isham, Norman M., and Albert F. Brown. *Early Connecticut Houses: An Historical and
    Architectural Study.* Providence, RI: Preston and Rounds, 1900.

————. *Early Rhode Island Houses: An Historical and Architectural Study.* Providence,
    RI: Preston and Rounds, 1895.

SOCIAL STUDIES (RACE, CLASS, AND GENDER)

Bishir, Catherine. "Landmarks of Power: Building a Southern Past, 1885–1915." *Southern
    Cultures* 1, no. 1 (1993): 5–46.

Chappell, Edward, and Julie Richter. "Wealth and Houses in Post-Revolutionary Virginia."
    In *Exploring Everyday Landscapes: Perspectives in Vernacular Architecture*, VII,
    edited by Annmarie Adams and Sally McMurry, 3–22. Knoxville: The University of
    Tennessee Press, 1997.

Cohen, Lizabeth A. "Embellishing a Life of Labor: An Interpretation of the Material
    Culture of American Working-Class Homes, 1885–1915." In *Common Places:
    Readings in American Vernacular Architecture*, edited by Dell Upton and John
    Michael Vlach, 261–81. Athens: University of Georgia Press, 1986.

Kwolek-Folland, Angel. *Engendering Business: Men and Women in the Corporate
    Office, 1870–1930.* Baltimore: Johns Hopkins University Press, 1994.

Spain, Daphne. *Gendered Spaces.* Chapel Hill: University of North Carolina Press, 1992.

Upton, Dell. "Black and White Landscapes in Eighteenth Century Virginia." In *Material Life in America, 1600–1860,* edited by Robert Blair St. George, 357–370. Boston: Northeastern University Press, 1988.

Vlach, John Michael. *Back of the Big House: The Architecture of Plantation Slavery.* Chapel Hill: The University of North Carolina Press, 1993.

Weisman, Leslie Kanes. *Discrimination by Design: A Feminist Critique of the Man-Made Environment.* Urbana: University of Illinois Press, 1992.

CULTURAL AND SYMBOLIC STUDIES

Glassie, Henry. *Folk Housing in Middle Virginia: A Structural Analysis of Historic Artifacts.* Knoxville: University of Tennessee Press, 1975.

St. George, Robert Blair. *Conversing by Signs: Poetics of Implication in Colonial New England Culture.* Raleigh: University of North Carolina Press, 1998.

Anthologies of Vernacular Architecture Articles

These anthologies collect significant scholarship on vernacular architecture topics that was first published in specialized journals or presented at conferences; the anthology gives the work a longer life and directs it to a broader audience.

Carter, Thomas, ed. *Images of an American Land: Vernacular Architecture in the Western United States.* Albuquerque: University of New Mexico Press, 1997.

Carson, Cary, Ronald Hoffman, and Peter J. Albert, eds. *Of Consuming Interests: The Style of Life in the Eighteenth Century.* Charlottesville and London: United States Capitol Historical Society and University Press of Virginia, 1994.

St. George, Robert B., ed. *Material Life in America, 1600–1860.* Boston: Northeastern University Press, 1988.

Upton, Dell, and John Vlach, eds. *Common Places: Readings in American Vernacular Architecture.* Athens: University of Georgia Press, 1986.

Journals and Collections of Essays

PERSPECTIVES IN VERNACULAR ARCHITECTURE

Perspectives in Vernacular Architecture (PVA), published as a series of books (usually every other year) from 1984 to 2005, compiled articles based on significant research presented at the annual meetings of the Vernacular Architecture Forum (VAF). The contents of these volumes are diverse and wide-ranging, covering national and international locations, time periods from the seventeenth century to the present, methods, and theories; articles were written by scholars from a broad range of disciplines.

Students of vernacular architecture will want to check every volume, which are listed below in order of volume number.

Note: In 2004, PVA began publication as an annual journal to replace the book-format volumes; volume 11, edited by Jan Jennings and Pamela Simpson, is the first issue in the new format. The journal will contain articles not only from the VAF meetings but also other articles reflecting the latest research in the field.

Wells, Camille, ed. *Perspectives in Vernacular Architecture,* I. Columbia: University of Missouri Press, 1984.

———. *Perspectives in Vernacular Architecture,* II. Columbia: University of Missouri Press, 1986.

Carter, Thomas, and Bernard L. Herman, eds. *Perspectives in Vernacular Architecture,* III. Columbia: University of Missouri Press, 1989.

———. *Perspectives in Vernacular Architecture,* IV. Columbia: University of Missouri Press, 1991.

Cromley, Elizabeth Collins, and Carter L. Hudgins, eds. *Gender, Class and Shelter*: *Perspectives in Vernacular Architecture,* V. Knoxville: University of Tennessee Press, 1995.

Hudgins, Carter L., and Elizabeth Collins Cromley, eds. *Shaping Communities: Perspectives in Vernacular Architecture,* VI. Knoxville: University of Tennessee Press, 1997.

Adams, Annmarie, and Sally McMurry, eds. *Exploring Everyday Landscapes*: *Perspectives in Vernacular Architecture,* VII. Knoxville: University of Tennessee Press, 1997.

McMurry, Sally, and Annmarie Adams, eds. *People, Power, Places*: *Perspectives in Vernacular Architecture,* VIII. Knoxville: University of Tennessee Press, 2000.

Hoagland, Alison K., and Kenneth A. Breisch, eds. *Constructing Image, Identity, and Place*: *Perspectives in Vernacular Architecture,* IX. Knoxville: University of Tennessee Press, 2003.

Breisch, Kenneth, and Alison Hoagland, eds. *Building Environments: Perspectives in Vernacular Architecture,* X. Knoxville: University of Tennessee Press, 2005.

JOURNALS OF PARTICULAR INTEREST

Journal of American Folklore
Journal of the Association for Preservation Technology
Journal of Design History
Journal of the Society of Architectural Historians
Landscape
Material Culture
Material Culture (Pioneer America Society)
Material History Review
Pioneer America
Winterthur Portfolio

Index

Invitation to Vernacular Architecture was designed and typeset on a Macintosh computer system using QuarkXPress software. The body text is set in 10/13 ITC Garamond and display type is also ITC Garamond. This book was manufactured by Thomson-Shore, Inc.